UNSEEN POWERS

UNSEEN POWERS
Realities of Our Relation to the Spiritual Realm

EVERETT LEADINGHAM, Editor

Though this book is designed for group study, it is also intended for personal enjoyment and spiritual growth. A leader's guide is available from your local bookstore or your publisher.

Beacon Hill Press of Kansas City
Kansas City, Missouri

Copyright 1999
by Beacon Hill Press of Kansas City

ISBN: 083-411-805X

Printed in the United States of America

Editor: Everett Leadingham
Assistant Editor: Charlie L. Yourdon
Executive Editor: Randy Cloud
Editorial Committee: Philip Baisley, Randy Cloud, Everett Leadingham, Thomas
Mayse, Larry Morris, Darlene Teague, Charlie L. Yourdon

Cover design: Ted Ferguson

10   9   8   7   6   5   4   3   2

Contents

A quick trip to your neighborhood bookstore will confirm the fact. People today are being drawn more and more to an understanding of the spiritual side of the world and of their own lives. Some have characterized the present generation as one of the most "spiritually inclined" cultures in recent centuries. But don't let the word "spiritual" fool you. Today's explorer of the spiritual domain is not restricted only to the traditional categories of religious spirituality. Today's spiritual topics run the gamut from meditation in the martial arts to channeling through the use of crystals. Many of these would-be spiritual travelers may be wrong in their methods and conclusions, but they are absolutely right in one thing—all humans have a distinctly spiritual side to our existence, a dimension to our lives that is essential to recognize. The Christian knows this is true for two related reasons. First, we read that "God is spirit, and his worshipers must worship in spirit and in truth" (John 4:24). And second, we recall the familiar words from Genesis 1:26, "Then God said, 'Let us make man in our image, in our likeness.'" God is Spirit, and we have been created in that same image. At the core of who God is and who He has created us to be lies the concept of spirit. So how do we go about discovering "our spiritual side"? The first place to start our journey into the unseen powers of this world, into the spiritual realities of life, is to explore what it means when we talk about God's Spirit, known as the Holy Spirit.

CHAPTER 1

The Holy Spirit: Our Soul's Thirst

by Dan Boone

BOB WILEY IS NEEDY. If his name sounds familiar to you, you've probably seen the video *What About Bob?* Bob has every ailment imaginable. Every phobia. Every complex. He has driven his psychiatrist out of the profession, and the psychiatrist decides to refer Bob to his least-liked competitor, Dr. Leo Marvin.

Dr. Marvin is the proud author of the recently released book *Baby Steps*. In his first session with Bob, Dr. Marvin successfully gets Bob to take a few baby steps of responsible action. Bob experiences the exhilaration of hope and decides that Dr. Marvin is the miracle worker he has been looking for all his life. The only problem—Dr. Marvin is about to go on a month-long vacation, and Bob will have to wait until he returns to proceed with therapy.

Bob is not one to wait patiently. He tries everything to discover where Dr. Marvin is vacationing and, following multiple failed attempts, succeeds. As Bob arrives in the quaint lake village, Dr. Marvin is exiting the local grocery store with his family. They meet face-to-face. Dr. Marvin rebuffs Bob sternly and tries to put him back on the bus. But Bob stands there declaring the pivotal words of the story, "I need, I need, I need."

Bob has discovered something about himself. His soul. The Hebrew word *nephesh* occurs 755 times in the Old Testament and is usually translated "soul." But there are other flavorings of the word that give us its fuller meaning.

It can mean "throat"—the primary organ for receiving air and water, the part of us that must remain open lest we die, the part of us that opens itself to life-sustaining substances.

It can mean "neck"—the most vulnerable part of our bodies. Ask Christopher Reeve about the seriousness of neck injury. When we speak of being endangered, we say our neck is in the noose.

It can mean "desire"—as in wanting something that lies outside us. *Nephesh* can mean longing, striving, wanting, thirsting.

These meanings define "soul" as needy, thirsty, open, vulnerable. When Bob Wiley says, "I need, I need, I need," he is expressing soul.

In the Old Testament, the soul is described as frightened, despaired, disquieted, weak, despondent, exhausted, defenseless, afflicted, troubled, and distressed. All this in the one whose creation is spoken of in Genesis 2:7 (KJV), "And the LORD God formed man of the dust of the ground, and breathed into his nostrils the breath of life; and man became a living soul *[nephesh]*."

The human being—a living thirst, an open throat, a vulnerable neck, a deep desire, a need.

If this is a definition of humanity, who is God? And how do we experience God? Genesis 2:7 (KJV) answers that question with another Hebrew word we need to notice: *ruach*. "And the LORD God formed man of the dust of the ground, and breathed into his nostrils the breath *[ruach]* of life; and man became a living soul *[nephesh]*."

When God breathes, creation begins. Has it occurred to you that God "breathes"? Breath is His domain. It comes from Him and returns to Him. Our need connects us to His breath. We are born with open windpipes waiting for something from the outside to animate us. God's breath coincides with our windpipes. The Hebrew word for God's Spirit, *ruach,* is pronounced ROO-ahck. The *ahck* needs to come out as if you're clearing your throat. Kind of a hard German sound. Shove air across your vocal cords so forcefully that breath is projected. The word for breath needs forceful breath just to say it.

Ruach means moving of air, wind, storm. This is the word used to speak of God's Spirit. The *ruach* of God sustains life, empowers people to do extraordinary things, deals with evil, and offers us a hopeful future. That's a lot to expect from the wind—unless that wind is holy wind, holy *ruach,* the Holy Spirit. That's what the word means—spirit. The Holy Spirit is the moving, empowering, life-giving, evil-cleansing, hope-promising, heart-activating breath of God. The Spirit of God (*ruach*) and the need of humans (*nephesh*) are meant to merge. But just how do we experience God as Spirit?

God's Spirit Sustains Life

Our Old Testament friend Job felt impelled to remind God of that fact. He said some choice things to God about his breath: "Remember, O God, that my life is but a breath" (7:7). "He would not let me regain my breath" (9:18) (which might well be interpreted, "God, you're standing on my windpipe!"). And he vowed to keep up the conversation with God "as long as I have life within me, the breath of God in my nostrils" (27:3).

The Spirit of the living God sustains all created life. It was the Spirit of God that hovered over the formless, empty, dark chaos in Genesis 1:1-2. It was the Spirit of God that placed breath in the first human. Idols cannot do this. Stars, stones, and soothsayers can't do this. God is the unequaled Creator and Sustainer of life. Humans are perfectly created to receive the breath of God and are sustained alive by the Spirit of God.

Job knew that his life was sustained by God. So did the psalmists who said with regularity that life is but a breath. The people of God lived with a consciousness that, if God held His breath, life would cease.

When Jeremiah chided the people for turning from God to idols, he reminded them that the idols were breathless. They were wood, stone, and iron. They had no breath in them to give their followers. Why would anyone in their right mind turn from the living God, full of life-giving breath, to idols who can't even breathe for themselves?

Truly, the Spirit of the living God sustains all created life.

God's Spirit Empowers People to Do Extraordinary Things

Samson killed hundreds of Philistines when the Spirit of God came upon him.

Joseph told Pharaoh what his dreams meant by the insight of the Spirit.

Craftsmen built the Tabernacle under the influence of God's breath.

Deborah became a charismatic military leader, rallying the people to fight by the power of the Spirit.

Daniel told Nebuchadnezzar what he had been dreaming in the palace king bed because of his Spirit-given insights.

Isaiah, Jeremiah, and Ezekiel prophesied when God breathed on them.

The Spirit of God came mightily upon people, clothed them, descended on them, entered them, impelled them. God's breath empowered people to do extraordinary things. God reveals himself as One who comes to help. The Spirit of God is on the move on behalf of needy beings. His power is unequaled.

God's Spirit Dealt with Evil

When God got angry, the Bible tells us He "snorted." Imagine a bull on a cold day, getting ready to attack. See the hot air being expelled from his nose? That's the Old Testament word used to describe the anger of God against evil. A hot fierce blast through the nostrils. Other descriptions are just as picturesque: a rushing torrent, a stream of burning sulfur, a strong wind bringing in a locust plague, a scorching wind blowing in from the desert, a driving wind swirling down on the wicked.

God's judgment is pictured as a violent storm before which no human can stand. Before the windstorm of God, we are like tumbleweed in a gale, a straw hut in a hurricane, a canoe in a typhoon. We don't stand a chance of coming out intact.

God's Spirit deals with evil. When we feel conviction for our wrong, we can be certain that God is moving to deal with us. The Holy Spirit convicts us of sin and brings the judgment of God to bear on evil.

God's Spirit Brings Hope About Our Future

When Old Testament people found themselves in desperate situations, God moved to offer them a future. He breathed upon the prophets, and they began talking about a Messiah. Here, at last, in a "bad news" world was some good news.

Isaiah said, "A shoot will come up from the stump of Jesse; from his roots a Branch will bear fruit. The Spirit of the LORD will rest on him—the Spirit of wisdom and understanding, the Spirit of counsel and of power, the Spirit of knowledge and of the fear of the LORD" (11:1-2).

And in Isaiah 61:1-3 this Messiah is pictured making a speech: "The Spirit of the Sovereign LORD is on me, because the LORD has anointed me to preach good news to the poor. He has sent me to bind up the brokenhearted, to proclaim freedom for the captives and release from darkness for the prisoners, to proclaim the year of the LORD's favor and the day of vengeance of our God, to comfort all who mourn, and provide for those who grieve in Zion."

The hopes of God's people rested on a Messiah who would be energized by the Spirit of God. However, it didn't end there. The Spirit would do something *inside* them. "I will sprinkle clean water on you, and you will be clean; I will

cleanse you from all your impurities and from all your idols
[which have no breath in them]. I will give you a new heart
and put a new spirit in you; I will remove from you your heart
of stone and give you a heart of flesh. And I will put my Spirit
in you and move you to follow my decrees and be careful to
keep my laws" (Ezekiel 36:25-27).

Their hope of a future was wrapped up in a God-breathed
Messiah, who would occupy the human heart as Spirit. To understand the work of the Holy Spirit today, we must understand Jesus as the model Spirit-filled Servant of God.

The Spirit of God sustains life, empowers people to do
extraordinary things, deals with evil, and offers us a hopeful
future. That's a lot to expect from the wind. Unless that wind
is holy wind, holy *ruach*, the Holy Spirit.

The Holy Spirit in the New Testament

As we move from the Old Testament into the New Testament, words change from Hebrew to Greek, but the concept
of the Holy Spirit as the Breath of God remains. The Gospels
tell us the good news that, in Jesus, God has breathed. Jesus
initiates His ministry on the platform of Isaiah 61, by telling
His hometown friends that the Spirit of the Sovereign Lord is
upon Him.

Everything Jesus does has to do with the Spirit. The Spirit came upon Him in visible form at His baptism. The Spirit
led Him into the wilderness to be tempted. The Spirit anointed Him to preach good news to the poor, to bind up the brokenhearted, to proclaim freedom for captives.

Jesus is the walking, talking, life-bringing Spirit of God.
When He died on the Cross, the Gospels say He breathed His
last and gave up His spirit (breath). But not for long.

Following His resurrection, "on the evening of that first
day of the week, when the disciples were together, with the
doors locked for fear of the Jews, Jesus came and stood among
them and said, 'Peace be with you!' After he said this, he
showed them his hands and side. The disciples were over-

joyed when they saw the Lord. Again Jesus said, 'Peace be with you! As the Father has sent me, I am sending you.' And with that he breathed on them and said, 'Receive the Holy Spirit'" (John 20:19-22).

On another occasion, the gift of the Holy Spirit was described as a rushing mighty wind. God stormed them with His Spirit.

As Jesus prepared His disciples to receive the Holy Spirit, we are invited to take a firsthand look at the Trinity in action. After telling the disciples that He was going away and that they were to carry on the work that He had been doing, He spoke to them about the Father, himself, and the Holy Spirit (the Helper):

> And I will ask the Father, and he will give you another Counselor [Helper] to be with you forever—the Spirit of truth. The world cannot accept him, because it neither sees him nor knows him. But you know him, for he lives with you and will be in you. I will not leave you as orphans; I will come to you. Before long, the world will not see me anymore, but you will see me. Because I live, you also will live. On that day you will realize that I am in my Father, and you are in me, and I am in you. . . . If anyone loves me, he will obey my teaching. My Father will love him, and we will come to him and make our home with him. . . . But the Counselor [Helper], the Holy Spirit, whom the Father will send in my name, will teach you all things and will remind you of everything I have said to you (*John 14:16-20, 23, 26*).

The intimacy of the Trinity is unmistakable. The Father is in the Son; the Son is in the Father. They together will come to make their home in believers and will be experienced as the Holy Spirit. The Holy Spirit is the Breath of Creator God, the Presence of God the Risen Christ, and the Empowerment of God the Helper.

If we understand ourselves to be needy souls, open throats, then the Holy Spirit is the way we experience God coming to us. He reveals himself as the moving, empowering, life-giving, evil-cleansing, hope-promising, heart-activating presence of God.

As you read the following chapters, my prayer is that you will experience the Holy Spirit as your life. The shoddy offerings of the world pale in comparison to the Breath of Life.

Background Scripture: Genesis 1:1-2; 2:7; Job 7:7; 9:18; 27:3; Isaiah 11:1-2; 61:1-3; Ezekiel 36:25-27; John 14:16-20, 23, 26; 20:19-22

About the Author: Dr. Dan Boone is senior pastor of College Church of the Nazarene in Bourbonnais, Illinois.

We have seen that God is indeed Spirit and that He has created humans in that same image. But what does it mean to be "created in the image of God"? It is obvious that we have bodies and that we also have minds. How are these two dimensions of our existence related to our "spiritual" side? Why is it important in this day of scientific fact and hard data to discuss that which we cannot touch or see? One has condescendingly described those who seek out the aspects of our lives that fall into strictly spiritual categories as a "metaphysical stroll through the dark, where the only discoveries we will find are the bumps and bruises that accompany all who wander aimlessly without the aid of their physical senses." In this chapter we will discover that our spiritual side is very important to our total identity as God's children and that there is adequate light at the end of the tunnel to guide our exploration.

CHAPTER 2

Humans as Spiritual Beings

by Joseph W. Seaborn

THE LITTLE BOY SAT WATCHING the TV program on endangered species. At the end, he was unusually silent. His mother quizzed him on his quietness. "Mother," he asked, "am I an endangered species?" "I don't think so," reassured his mother. "Why do you ask?" The boy responded, "Because you take such good care of me. The TV said that we have to take care of endangered species or they will become extinct. There's only one of me, and if you didn't take care of me, then I would be extinct!"

You can't get three chapters into the Bible before you are overwhelmed with God's infinite care for His ultimate creation—humans. Two-thirds of the creation account focuses on humans, with the other third focusing on everything else. It's an illustration of God's priorities. He made all the rest of creation to look at, but humans He made to know. And not just humans as a blob of humanity, but each of us in turn He created for a face-to-face encounter with himself. Each of us is important. Each of us is a unique creation. The little boy was more right than he knew. Each of us is so rare and so valuable that God never wants us to stray far from His care and protection.

A Breath of Fresh Air

Genesis is both the first book and the best book in the Bible for helping us see where we came from, who we are, and where we need to go. The striking role of human beings in God's creation is clear from the start. In Genesis 1:11, God commands, "Let the land produce vegetation." Nine verses later He continues, "Let the water teem with living creatures, and let birds fly above the earth across the expanse of the sky" (v. 20). The next stanza of the creation epic keeps up the creative pace, "Let the land produce living creatures according to their kinds: livestock, creatures that move along the ground, and wild animals, each according to its kind" (Genesis 1:24). It's as if God has struck a cadence. He's on a roll. His creativity is flowing with every new round of creation, adding to His joy. You would fully expect it to reach a crescendo with the words, "Let the earth bring forth humankind . . ."

But those words never appear. Instead, the rhythm is broken by a whole new phrase that omits earth, sky, and seas as points of origin. A fifth grader could tell this "Let us" is different. "Then God said, '*Let us* make man in our image, in our likeness, and let them rule over the fish of the sea and the birds of the air, over the livestock, over all the earth, and over all the creatures that move along the ground.' So God created man in his own image, in the image of God he created him; male and female he created them" (Genesis 1:26-27, emphasis added). The very phrase "Let us make man" hints at our higher level of living. God was *happy* with the guppies and goldfish, seals and sea lions, turtles and toads. However, by the time you sing this seventh stanza in this creation hymn, He is *very happy.* All else was good, but humankind was *very* good.

Genesis 2:7 adds two vital details. It has the honor of telling us about the two key components of the human being, the body shaped from a hundred-plus pounds of dirt and the spirit poured directly from the breath of God into the handful of earth. The Hebrew word *neshamah* means a blast or gust of wind. So God blew a gust of divine breath into a handful of sacred soil and formed a *nephesh,* or a living soul. With this simple, single act, we became spiritual beings.

Each human being is a combination of the dust of the ground and God's breath. A lot of mental energy has been spent trying to sort out whether people are body and soul; or body, soul, and spirit; or some other combination. These first two positions carry the rather unwieldy labels of *dichotomy* (body and soul) and *trichotomy* (body, soul, and spirit). The discussion over which position—if either—is accurate has created its own set of verbal puzzles. In fact, the discussion has raged both inside and outside the church with both biblical and secular terms thrown about with equal vigor. The primary viewpoints are simple to summarize.

Persons as Atoms

A group of Greeks got lost in the philosophical woods and came up with the notion that humankind is nothing more than a clever combination of atoms. Men with names like Epicurus (341-270 B.C.) and Lucretius (96-55 B.C.) claimed that we are the joint venture of atoms and the empty spaces that circulate around them. They argued that soul and spirit were just words in space with no echo in reality. Plotinus (A.D. 205-270) came along and tried to dignify the error with a couplet, "Seek not the face of God to scan / the proper study of mankind is man." This view of humans as nothing more than a friendly flask of atoms has had a few subscribers in modern times, but common sense has made the followers few.

The modern philosopher David Hume (A.D. 1711-1776) held a variation of this view. He claimed that a person is a group of sensations without a true center of spiritual personhood. In his view, many animals would be superior to people, because animals often have superior senses of hearing, seeing, touching, tasting, or smelling.

Persons as Separate Compartments of Body and Spirit

Plato carried a lot of weight with his view that the human being is a union of two distinct substances—body and a reasoning spirit or intellect. He argued that the two never fully merge, so that the soul can later migrate to another body and be just as happy or happier in its new "hotel." This teaching feeds into the equally erroneous view of the reincarnation of souls. Plato is famous for the line, "The body is the prison house of the soul." Typical of his Greek worldview, he held a lower view of anything material, anything you could touch. To him, the spirit was so superior to the body that the two could never be one. His line of reasoning would say that the human being is two distinct and separate realities, like a bicycle and its rider or like a rower and the boat.

Paul had to come along in 1 Corinthians 15 and declare the biblical view that God made both body and spirit, and both would be with us forever. The spirit would be redeemed and the body transformed, but Paul would have no part of a philosophy that praised the spirit and denounced the body.

Persons as a Single Substance

Aristotle felt that the human being was a single substance that combined matter and spirit or material and immaterial. Aristotle went too far in arguing that humans were just a higher form of every other animal in the universe. His belief did not include the unique role of Jehovah God in the creative process.

Little errors at the beginning have serious consequences at the end. These three views had just enough truth to make them believable but not enough to make them biblical.

The question as to whether we are a kind of unified "twoness" or "threeness" is not finally resolved in the Bible. We should not be dogmatic about what the Bible has chosen not to make certain. There are passages that seem to suggest one or the other and a handful of passages that mention more. In an analogy, if you mix sodium (Na) and chlorine (Cl), you get salt (NaCl). Salt is not one of the two combining elements but a unique compound. If you mix hydrogen (H) with sulfur (S) and oxygen (O) in the right proportion, you get sulfuric acid (H_2SO_4), which is no longer three but one new compound. Whatever number of elements comprise our person, we may be sure that, except on days when we are "beside ourselves," we are, in fact, one person made in the beautiful image of God.

Persons as a Mixture of Flesh and Spirit

Genesis 2:7 teaches that God mixed dust and His divine breath into a combination that He called "a living soul." At least here in Genesis, *soul* refers to the combination as a whole, not just one of its parts. Here, where the story is told at its simplest, it is enough for us to be earth and breath, flesh and spirit, in a profound mystery of merger.

What we need to appreciate is that the Bible often uses a string of words to indicate the totality of the person. For example, when Jesus calls us to give full allegiance to His cause, He asks us to "Love the Lord your God with all your heart and with all your soul and with all your mind" (Matthew 22:37). This process of stringing terms together was one way by which the Hebrew language allowed a speaker or writer to indicate the whole. We would do the same today if we said, "The fire burned the whole school—classrooms, offices, gym, and storage sheds." The Hebrew language did not have a single term that expressed wholeness; therefore, it resorted to a short list in order to get at the whole. To take each item by itself would be to miss the spirit of the verse. Jesus simply meant to love God through and through. It is not accidental that you will never find one of these short lists anywhere in Scripture that does not include the spiritual dimension as a key component of the total person.

Mirroring the Image of God

There are two main teachings as to how our individual souls come into existence. From the very first century of the Christian church, these two views have been offered to explain the instant of our origin. *Traducianism* (from a Latin word meaning "to carry across or to carry through") holds that we get our souls from the union of our parents. God has so designed us that, in the act of procreation, a new spirit is created to energize the miniature body that is simultaneously formed. *Creationism,* on the other hand, teaches that God performs a fresh creative act for every baby at the time of conception.[1]

Whole shelves of books are stacked up to argue each side. Creationists say that verses such as Psalm 33:15, Isaiah 57:16, Jeremiah 38:16, and Zechariah 12:1 support this view. The Traducian camp leans on the passage that says that God rested from His creation on the seventh day (Genesis 2:2) and from that time to this has primarily allowed the God-created process of birth through plants, animals, and human beings to continue the creative process. Plus, if you hold the creationist view, the Traducians would assert that God creates a defective sinful soul each time a child is conceived.

This argumentation and these distinctions seem at times rather fruitless. I believe that at conception, the image of God is once again allowed to take up residence in human life. Be it ever so tiny, a growing fetus is already the temple of the most high God (1 Corinthians 6:19). His spirit has already reached out to embrace the new spirit that the God-ordained act of procreation has produced.

As that child is born and matures through the years, it demonstrates a number of features that mark it as distinctively spiritual.

A Yearning for Relationship

No person ever begins as a self-formed, self-sustaining packet. At the time of our personal conception, our two parents, and then we, were present at this act of cocreation. The trinity, or threeness, of persons in God is mirrored in our own earthly trinity—a man, a woman, and a child.

The being of God is a relational being—three persons in a loving and complete unity. Just like the trinity of God, we, too, are beings in relationship. We are designed to bond and belong to one another. The Bible calls us to relate in two directions, vertical and horizontal. Too many people try to work out a sense of themselves and then turn to the spiritual component of their lives as a kind of appendix. But that view misses a whole segment of reality. To deny ourselves a relationship with God is to deny ourselves. To affirm that vertical relationship is to affirm ourselves. We sometimes meet persons who call themselves "humanists." By that, they mean that they hold humans as the measure of all things. But if humans are put at the center of life, life is dehumanized. Only a relationship with God gives us the potential of true humanness. In that sense, the only true "humanist" is a Christian.

The call to social interconnectedness is imbedded in Christ's high-priestly prayer, "That all of them may be one, Father, just as you are in me and I am in you. May they also be in us" (John 17:21). Our relationships only reflect the community of the Godhead. We need each other in order to be our fullest selves. Our yearning for God is one of God's greatest gifts to us. We have a God-shaped vacuum in our hearts, and the shape of the vacuum is divine.

In the Greek, there are two words used for "person." One is *atomon,* which denotes the person as a unit, turned inward, self-contained, isolated, a number recorded in a census. The other word, *prosopon,* literally translates "face" and refers to the person looking outward to others, in relationship, involved in community. *Atomon* signifies separation; *prosopon* signifies communion. There is no surer sign of our spiritual dimension than the fact that we are happier and healthier when we live as a *prosopon* and not as an *atomon.*

In our dehumanized world where it is hard and usually awkward to look each other in the face, we need to reaffirm the supreme value of direct personal interaction. This touching of spirit with spirit is as near as we come to imitating the trinity of God. In its essence, holiness is holding our spirits so close to God's Spirit that, as Augustine once put it, our will becomes so lost in God's will that we cannot tell the difference between the two.

A Chance to Choose

In mirroring God, we also have the privilege of choice. If God wanted to, He could choose to send the righteous to hell and sinners to heaven. He chooses not to do that, but He could. In our likeness to God, we can choose too. We can choose to go to hell when we were made for heaven. Hopefully, none of us will make this decision, but hell *is* a choice.

Part of our mystery is our mastery over choices. Just as God chose to create human beings, so humans can choose to worship God. The very process of creation secured our likeness to God. This does not mean that God is little more than a magnified human or that a human is a miniature God, but it does mean that God is all that humans are—and infinitely more. Any essential quality we have in our humanness is first found in God. That includes our privilege of choice.

It is a breathtaking thought that God gave us so much power of choice. We have the stunning ability to either run *to* Him or run *from* Him.

A Capacity to Communicate

God and Adam talked. Even after Adam sinned and lost his perfect harmony with God, they were still in conversation. When God asked Adam his whereabouts, Adam tried to hide. Still, God persisted: "'Where are you?' He answered, 'I heard you in the garden, and I was afraid because I was naked; so I hid'" (Genesis 3:9-10). Not only was Adam able to talk with God, but also he sensed in his heart a sudden maladjustment to God, a sense of being alienated.

Our ability to spend time with God and enjoy His company is what gives us supreme worth. God did not say to Adam, "Unless you make four more fig-leaf skirts by tomorrow afternoon, I'll have to fire you and make me a new man." Rather, God said something like, "Adam, come, let's go walking in the garden in the cool of the day." It was his walking with God, and not a dresser drawer full of fig-leaf skirts, that gave Adam his value. Our worth to God is based on our spiritual communion with Him and not on our productivity in His world. In our materialism-soaked society, we are tempted to be humans *doing* before we are human *beings*. Personal worth in our culture is based on the thickness of our wallet and not on our nearness to God.

God is happy to have us working for Him, but His supreme joy is to have us communing with Him. I'll take my 12-year-old in a rich and wide-ranging conversation any day over her cleaning her room! Although if you could see her room . . .

A Unique Place in His Plan

It is not enough to say that human beings as a group are special. We must also affirm that within the human family each individual possesses a beautiful uniqueness. Each of us is a priceless treasure not to be found anywhere else. We are not interchangeable memory chips on a computer board. In each of us, God has placed plans that can't be realized by anyone else in the universe. Our inner uniqueness of spirit is mirrored in our faces. Every human face is different. It is astounding what God has achieved by way of individual faces with only a few square inches to work with. How much more can He do when working with the infinite variations of memory, background, gifts, and preferences that lie hidden in our hearts?

The Bible assigns our origin to a specific command by God. One of the strongest arguments against evolution is the fact that Eve was formed from Adam's side, not from a series of sample persons whom God made just to test the model. The human family descended from precisely two human beings. Neither Adam nor Eve were evolutionary products. Their uniqueness points to our own.

To emphasize our uniqueness right into eternity, Revelation 2:17 states that Jesus will give each of us who conquers a white stone, and on that stone will be written a new name that no one knows except the one who receives it. That means our spiritual uniqueness will inhabit both time and eternity. In fact, most of our life won't be spent on earth.

It is obvious from this group of ideas that the image of God is not so much something that we have as something that we are. It's not as if God made humans and then wrapped His image around their arms like WWJD bracelets.[2] Humans are the image of God. First Corinthians 11:7 says that we are the image and glory of God. It is a higher calling than most of us realize.

Pilgrims in Process

The image of God in humans, though it may be marred, cannot die. If it is God's image, it is by definition eternal, permanent. In Adam, the image was defaced but not erased.

Whatever the Fall in the Garden of Eden did to the human family, it did not reduce us to stupid, spirit-absent creatures. After Adam's sin, Adam was still Adam. He was still a person, still reasonable, still capable of choices and reflection. Sin did not eradicate the image of God; it only caused it to malfunction.

It may seem odd, but we would not even be sinners in need of salvation were it not for our being in the image of God. To sin we must be able to choose. That capacity to choose marks us uniquely as spiritual beings.

If this chapter shows us anything, it highlights our similarity to God, how close our own personality is to His. For too long our emphasis has been on the differences between God and ourselves. For balance we would do well to emphasize for a time our nearness and likeness to God. Over the last several decades we have suffered, not from intimacy with God, but from the remoteness of God. To a great many in our time, He is little more than a shadowy energy far away in a cloudy heaven. He is thought of as part of a dim and distant dream world that is wrapped in thick mystery.

That idea of God makes prayer seem like a difficult chore at best and an impossible communication at worst. Even in our earthly relationships, the frequency and length of interaction is usually influenced by the distance the communication has to travel. We all know that a phone call across 4,000 miles arrives within the same second as a phone call across town, but which call will we make more quickly? Which phone number will we call more often? Even if money were no object, we still feel closer to a person who is physically closer to us.

It makes all the difference when we realize that God is not far away in a mysterious shadow land but near at hand. His Spirit is not covered by a canopy and hidden to our heart. He is immediately beside us, His Spirit forever brushing against our spirit.

This should not cause us to become overly chummy with God. This is no call to parade our own ego. After all, "EGO" means: Edging God Out. Rabbi Bunam used to tell his disciples, "Everyone must have two pockets, so that he can reach into the one or the other, according to his needs. In his right pocket are to be the words, 'For my sake the world was created' and in the left pocket, 'I am earth and ashes.'"[3] Such is the human paradox. We are a strange mixture of glory and ashes.

God has finished with the animals. They are no longer in His workshop. Even if He plans for animals to survive death and live in paradise with us, they cannot have eternal life, because eternal life consists in knowing the only true God and Jesus Christ whom He has sent. That can only happen as our spirit relates with God's Spirit.

God has not finished with us. The animals may be finished; but with us, He's only just begun. He keeps on carving and shaping us into His image. We remain in the workshop. Because we are spirit, He continues to refine and mature us. We have our share of human nature. We know in a heartbeat when we have disappointed God. But we also know in our hearts when our spirit has touched His Spirit with joy. And when we examine our own spirit and celebrate its marvelous capacity to know God directly, we can say of our spirit what David said of our body, it, too, is "fearfully and wonderfully made" (Psalm 139:14).

1. The term "creationism" is being used here in its historical context, not in reference to modern scientific debates about the formation of the world.

2. WWJD = "What Would Jesus Do?"

3. Martin Buber, *Tales of the Hasidim, The Early Masters* (New York: Schocken, 1968), 1:282.

Background Scripture: Genesis 1:11, 20, 24, 26-27; 2:2, 7; 3:9-10; Psalms 33:15; 139:14; Isaiah 57:16; Jeremiah 38:16; Zechariah 12:1; Matthew 22:37; John 17:21; 1 Corinthians 6:19; 11:7; 15:35-44

About the Author: Dr. Joseph Seaborn is senior pastor of College Wesleyan Church in Marion, Indiana. He is the author of numerous magazine articles and seven books. He has written and produced a seven-part video series titled *The Genesis Plan for Family Living.* Dr. Seaborn is married to Dr. Mary Seaborn, who teaches at Indiana Wesleyan University. They have three children.

In one of the most spine-tingling and faith-inspiring passages to be found in the entire Bible, we learn that what first meets the eye is not always a true reflection of reality. In 2 Kings 6, we read the mighty king of Aram was at war with Israel. The mightier prophet Elisha was able to predict where the armies of Aram would attack next, and he warned the king of Israel in time for defensive action to be put in place. In a rage, the king of Aram sent a large task force with horses and chariots to capture the pesky prophet. When the army of Aram had surrounded Elisha, his servant cried out in fear, "Oh, my lord, what shall we do?" (v. 15). Elisha calmly replied to his Lord, God himself, "Open his eyes" (v. 17). And God showed the fearful servant a sight that all Christians should rejoice in: "He looked and saw the hills full of horses and chariots of fire all around Elisha" (v. 17). Elisha's commentary says it all: "Those who are with us are more than those who are with them" (v. 16). Assuming Elisha's heavenly army to be composed of angels, what do we make of this Old Testament passage? Is the world yet today filled with angelic beings, invisible to all but the most spiritually sensitive, who work on behalf of God's people? Let's see what the Scriptures teach us.

CHAPTER 3

What Angels Are Like

by Andrew J. Bandstra

WE CAN NEVER CONSIDER the "nature" of angels in the abstract, only in the context of the work they do. Angels are ambassadors in God's kingdom who take part in God's revelation throughout history.

It's important to keep this image of angels as Kingdom ambassadors in mind as we explore what the Bible reveals about these beings.

Spiritual Beings

In a passage comparing and contrasting angels with the eternal Son of God, the author of Hebrews concludes with a rhetorical question: "Are not all angels ministering spirits sent to serve those who will inherit salvation?" (Hebrews 1:14). It's a question that expects an affirmative response: "Yes, all angels are such ministering spirits."

There you have it: angels are *spirits* who *minister.*

Since angels are spirits, it's probable that they lack bodily form and are usually not visible to the physical eye. Note that Paul, in Colossians 1:16, seems to equate "things in heaven" with the things "invisible," which clearly refers to the principalities and powers (KJV).

Nevertheless in the Bible, angels often assume bodily shape to witness to God's gospel story. Consider these examples:

- Abraham *saw* three men standing near his tent under the great trees of Mamre (Genesis 18:1-2). Only later do we find out that they were angels from the Lord God who had a hand in the destruction of Sodom and Gomorrah (Genesis 19:1).

- When Nebuchadnezzar sent Shadrach, Meshach, and Abednego to the fiery furnace, a fourth person suddenly appeared in the fire who looked "like a son of the gods" (Daniel 3:13-27).
- The birth of Jesus was foretold to Mary by the angel Gabriel, who appeared to her in bodily form in her hometown of Nazareth (Luke 1:26-38).
- According to Mark's Gospel, the women entering the tomb "*saw* a young man dressed in a white robe sitting on the right side" (Mark 16:5, emphasis added).

However, these seem to be only temporary appearances on special occasions.

Created Beings

The Bible treats angels as part of the created order. In other words, they stand with us as created beings in contrast to God, who is the Creator. To be sure, angels are not mentioned in the accounts of creation given in the first three chapters of Genesis, so we have no account of *when* they were created.

It's important to keep in mind that angels are *created* beings, otherwise Christians might too quickly become superstitious and attribute to angels the glory that should be given to God alone. If people begin to think that angels are really the dispensers of blessings, they might quickly fall down and worship them.

In the Book of Revelation, John also seems concerned about people worshiping angels (angels do, after all, play a great role in that book). John says that after the angel gave him his commission to write, he [John] "fell at his feet to worship him" (19:10). But the angel reprimanded him: "Do not do it! I am a fellow servant with you and with your brothers who hold to the testimony of Jesus. Worship God!" Almost exactly the same experience is recounted in Revelation 22:8-9.

We are not to worship angels—God alone is worthy of our worship.

Limited Beings

The first two characteristics—that angels are *created* and that they are *spirits*—are the most important and basic of the descriptions the Bible gives us. The other three characteristics that we will look at in this chapter can be gathered from these first two.

In considering the evidence, we may not always get a consistent picture of angels in the Bible. For example, on the one hand, Jacob, while at Luz (later called Bethel), had a dream of a stairway or ladder stretching from earth to heaven. According to Genesis 28:12, the angels of God were ascending and descending on the ladder. On the other hand, some angels (cherubim and seraphim) are said to have wings, and these angels are said to "fly" (Daniel 9:21; Revelation 14:6). If angels fly, it is not easy to understand why they would need a ladder, is it? Yet, in one important way, these images (the ladder, wings, flying) agree: they all make clear that angels are limited with respect to space; they are not everywhere present.

Nor are angels all-powerful. As creatures, they operate by divine authority—they do what God commands them to do. The psalmist exhorts: "Praise the LORD, you his angels, you mighty ones who do his bidding, who obey his word" (Psalm 103:20).

Even though angels are heavenly creatures, they are also limited in their knowledge. Jesus says about the coming of the Son of Man: "No one knows about that day or hour, *not even the angels in heaven,* nor the Son, but only the Father" (Mark 13:32, emphasis added).

Peter says something to the same effect in 1 Peter 1:10-12. He magnifies the insight given to the prophets about the salvation that ultimately came through Jesus Christ and that was preached in the gospel. This discernment given to the prophets was so great that it surpassed the knowledge of angels, as Peter implies when he concludes: "even angels long to look into these things" (v. 12).

Holy Beings

Three times the New Testament refers to "holy angels" (Matthew 25:31 [KJV]; Luke 9:26; and Revelation 14:10). It is likely that Jesus (in Matthew and Luke) is simply describing one characteristic of all angels: they are beings who have been set aside to serve God. Holiness, here, does not refer so much to a moral quality as it does to separation for the service of God. Angels are creatures, as Psalm 103:20 reminds us, who do God's bidding and obey God's Word.

This reference to "holy" angels provides the occasion to note that we are discussing exclusively "good" angels. According to Christian tradition, "the devil and his angels" are really angels who through sin fell from their exalted place and became evil angels. The best evidence the Bible gives that the devil and his hosts are fallen angels is found in Jude and 2 Peter. Jude 6 says: "And the angels who did not keep their positions of authority but abandoned their own home." This verse has its parallel in 2 Peter 2:4: "For if God did not spare angels when they sinned." The biblical evidence for this view of Satan as a fallen angel is not overwhelming, yet it may be adequate.

Most of the time, however, when the Bible uses the term "angel" to refer to one or more extraterrestrial messengers, it is referring to "good" angels. These "good" angels, not the "evil" ones, are our focus.

Individualistic Beings

Humans, according to the Bible, are organically related to one another in that we are all descendants of one person, as Acts 17:26 and Romans 5:12-21 indicate. Furthermore, we are intimately related to a specific family because we are born from human parents who themselves come from parents, and so on.

Such organic relationships do not exist among angels. In Mark 12:25, in response to a question of the Sadducees about marriage in the resurrection, Jesus says: "When the dead rise, they will neither marry nor be given in marriage; they will be *like the angels in heaven*" (emphasis added). What seems to be underlying this teaching is the understanding that angels do not participate in marriage the way we humans do. There are no "little" angels who are born from other angels.

While there seem to be no "male" and "female" in the angelic world, all of the references to angels in the Bible seem to be male. "He" is the personal pronoun used, and the angels generally take on the bodily appearance of men when they are used to tell the gospel story of the coming of the Kingdom. The important thing to consider is that whatever commitment angels have to one another, their clear and total commitment is to the service of God and the revelation of the coming Kingdom.

Names and Titles: Angel

Both the Hebrew word *mal'akh* and the Greek word *angelos,* from which we get the word "angel," mean "messenger." These terms were used to refer to the messenger or the ambassador in human affairs, the one who spoke and acted as the representative of the one who sent him or her.

In the Bible, the term "angel" also sometimes describes human messengers, but more often it is used to speak of heavenly messengers. Angels are God's messengers who speak and act as His representatives.

Names and Titles: Cherubim and Seraphim

The singular of these words is "cherub" and "seraph," and the plural [in English] is either "cherubs" and "seraphs" or, more often in the Bible, following the Hebrew, "cherubim" and "seraphim."

The term "seraphim" is used only once in the Bible, in Isaiah 6:1-7, where we find an account of Isaiah's vision of the Lord, high and lifted up, seated on the throne, and the train of the Lord's robe filling the Temple. Above the throne were the seraphim—six-winged creatures, using a set of two wings for covering their faces, two for covering their feet, and two for flying. Chanting responsively, they announced the holiness of the Lord: "Holy, holy, holy is the LORD Almighty; the whole earth is full of his glory" (v. 3). So powerful was this announcement that it shook the doorposts of the Temple, filled the Temple with smoke, and greatly affected the prophet, who made a confession of his uncleanness. Then one of the seraphs brought a live coal from the altar and touched Isaiah's lips, declaring his guilt to be taken away and his sin atoned for. Here the seraphim have both a prophetic function of proclaiming God's holiness and a priestly function of cleansing the prophet's uncleanness, guilt, and sin.

The term "cherubim" occurs frequently in Scripture. We can distinguish four distinct but related kinds of occurrences:

- After sin had separated the original human pair from God, cherubim were stationed east of Eden with flashing swords to guard the way to the tree of life (Genesis 3:24).
- Cherubim, apparently two-winged creatures, were associated with the dwelling places of God—the Tabernacle and the later Solomonic Temple—in two ways:

  First, two cherubim were connected with the ark of the covenant in the holy of holies. In the Tabernacle they seem to be placed on top of the ark overlooking the mercy seat (Exodus 25:17-22). In the Solomonic Temple they were larger creatures, with wings stretching from side to side in the holy of holies, and the ark of the covenant was placed beneath them (1 Kings 6:23-28; 2 Chronicles 3:10-13). This association with the ark of the covenant became descriptive of the God of Israel as the one who "dwells" (NKJV) or is "enthroned between the cherubim" (1 Samuel 4:4; 2 Samuel 6:2; 2 Kings 19:15; 1 Chronicles 13:6; Psalm 80:1; 99:1; Isaiah 37:16).

Second, cherubim are mentioned in connection with the artwork in the Tabernacle, specifically in the veil separating the holy place from the holy of holies (Exodus 26:31-35; 2 Chronicles 3:14).

- Cherubim are pictured in a highly complex vision of Ezekiel. In Ezekiel 1, we read of four living creatures, each with four faces (of a man, a lion, an ox, and an eagle), four wings, and a wheel with eyes. In Ezekiel 10 we find what appears to be a similar vision, only now the living creatures are called cherubim, and they are associated with the glory of the Lord leaving the Temple.

- In John's description of his vision of God's throne room, he doesn't use the word "cherubim," but the four living creatures that he sees surrounding God's throne are much like Ezekiel's cherubim (see especially Revelation 4:6-11). As in other places in his vision, John sees images much like those given in the Old Testament but with peculiar differences. These living creatures do not have four faces, but each of them is like one of the faces of Ezekiel's living creature—one like a lion, one like an ox, one like an eagle, and one like a man. And instead of two wings or four wings, these creatures, like the seraphim of Isaiah 6, have six wings. It is also significant that these living creatures, similar to the seraphim of Isaiah 6, sing day and night: "Holy, holy, holy is the Lord God Almighty, who was, and is, and is to come" (v. 8).

Names and Titles: Archangels

This term, which literally means "chief angels," is used only twice in the Bible. In 1 Thessalonians 4:16, Paul says that accompanying the coming of the Lord from heaven will be three, probably related, powerful sounds: a loud command, the voice of an archangel, and the trumpet call of God. In Jude 9, an "archangel" is described who did not arrogantly presume power to himself in his dispute with the devil but said, "The Lord rebuke you!"

Though "archangel" means something like "chief angel," we should be careful not to read too much into this term and assume we can carefully distinguish and classify all the orders of angels. Medieval theologians alleged that there were nine orders of intermediate spirits (listed from highest to lowest in rank): seraphim, cherubim, thrones, dominions, virtues, powers, principalities, archangels, and angels. However, much of this ranking was apparently based on speculation. The Bible only mentions groupings of angels without specifying rank and numbers.

This is probably the most appropriate place to consider the two named angels, Michael and Gabriel. Just a word about their names. In Exodus 23:21, God tells Israel that he will send an angel with them on the way to the Promised Land, to whom they should indeed pay heed, "since my Name is in him." Reflecting that truth, *"El"* at the end of each name is the name of God in Hebrew. Thus we have Micha*el* and Gabri*el* (and in other Jewish literature, Rapha*el*, Uri*el*, Sari*el*, etc.). Michael probably means, "Who is like God?" and Gabriel means either "man of God" or "God is strong." (Raphael means "God has healed," and Uriel probably means "God is light.")

Michael is called an archangel in Jude 9. There, Michael is recognized for his modesty and restraint (unlike the leaders who were tyrannizing the church to whom Jude was writing). Michael appears in the Book of Daniel as the one who has a special task as the champion of Israel against the rival angel of the Persians (10:13, 20). In Daniel 12:1, he leads the heavenly armies against all supernatural forces of evil in the last great battle. This theme of Daniel 12:1 is taken up in Revelation 12:7-12, which describes the beginning of that great battle between Michael and his angels and the dragon (also identified as "that ancient serpent . . . the devil, or Satan") and his angels.

Gabriel also appears in Daniel, but primarily as a heavenly messenger (who makes his appearance like a man, Daniel 8:16; 9:21). He comes to interpret a vision that reveals the future and to give understanding and wisdom to Daniel himself (8:17; 9:22). In the New Testament, Gabriel is mentioned only in the birth narratives recorded in Luke 1. Here, too, he is primarily a heavenly messenger who brings good news and thus reveals the future.

Conclusion

Angels are created, spiritual beings who are limited in their power. Now that we know what angels are, we will explore in the next chapter how they serve God as His messengers.

Background Scripture: Genesis 3:24; 18:1-2; 28:12; Exodus 23:21; 25:17-22; 26:31-35; 1 Samuel 4:4; 2 Samuel 6:2; 1 Kings 6:23-28; 2 Kings 19:15; 1 Chronicles 13:6; 2 Chronicles 3:10-14; Ezekiel 1; 10; Psalms 80:1; 99:1; 103:20; Isaiah 6:1-7; 14:12; 37:16; Daniel 8:16-17; 9:21-22; 10:13; 10:20; 12:1; Matthew 25:31; 28:2-7; Mark 12:25; 13:32; 16:5; Luke 1:11-20, 26-37; 9:26; Acts 17:26; Romans 5:12-21; Colossians 1:16; Hebrews 1:14; 1 Thessalonians 4:16; 1 Peter 1:10-12; 2 Peter 2:4; Jude 6, 9; Revelation 4:6-11; 12:7-12; 14:6-10; 19:10; 22:8-9

Recently I was in a restaurant, sitting quietly in my booth, munching my morning muffin. On the other side of the partition, in a booth of their own, I could hear two women in conversation. While the partition was high enough to block our view of each other, it did nothing to diminish my ability to hear every word they spoke. Without trying to eavesdrop, I allowed myself to tune in to their interesting discussion: "Did you know that everyone has a personal guardian angel?"

"No, I didn't."

"And everyone's guardian angel is someone that person knew in life, a friend or relative who has died."

"You mean that my guardian angel could be my recently departed grandmother?"

"It's entirely possible!"

What is the truth about angels? Popular secular culture has certainly latched onto the idea that angels are at work in our lives, but what does Scripture tell us?

CHAPTER 4

Messengers of God

by Andrew J. Bandstra

WE LEARNED IN THE LAST CHAPTER a little about the nature of angels. Now it remains to talk about the functions and ministry of angels.

Earthly Representatives

Sometimes when we think of messengers, we have a rather strong conviction that they are really unimportant. "Only a messenger" we often say—as if messengers were sort of office "errand boys" or "gofers" who are low on the pay scale and have little responsibility other than to bring written notes or oral requests from one person to another.

But even a quick survey of how the Hebrew word for "messenger" (mal'akh) is used in the Old Testament should disabuse us of this light understanding of the term. It clearly refers to a very responsible person, a kind of ambassador who represents in speech and action the one who sent him or her. This special sense of "envoy" aptly represents the first time the term is used to designate in one passage both the heavenly messengers from God and those earthly messengers sent by Jacob to secure the favor of Esau (Genesis 32:1-3).

Other examples underscore the responsible role of the earthly messengers: Messengers often represent a king, such as Saul in 1 Samuel 16:19. A prophet is sometimes called the Lord's messenger—one who gives the Lord's message to the people (Haggai 1:13) or who will prepare the way before the Lord (Malachi 3:1). Twice the priest is called a messenger from the Lord (Malachi 2:7 and Ecclesiastes 5:6, NKJV).

So a human messenger *(mal'akh)* was a responsible representative of the sender—and so, too, were the angels as messengers of the Lord. In the New Testament, the word *angelos* refers to an earthly messenger only six times. Three times it is used in quoting Malachi 3:1 as being fulfilled in John the Baptist (Matthew 11:10; Mark 1:2; Luke 7:27). Once it is used of messengers from John the Baptist to Jesus (Luke 7:24) and once of messengers sent by Jesus to prepare His way toward Jerusalem (Luke 9:52). In James 2:25, the Greek word for "messengers" is used (NIV: "spies") for the men whom Rahab hid by faith. In the other 169 instances where it appears in the New Testament, *angelos* refers to a heavenly messenger or "angel."

Like human messengers, angels never speak or act simply on their own. They only and always speak for and act in behalf of God.

Perhaps no passage in the Bible speaks as clearly as Exodus 23:20-22 of the close relationship between an angel and his Sender. God says: "See, I am sending an angel ahead of you to guard you along the way and to bring you to the place I have prepared. Pay attention to him and listen to what he says . . . and do all that I say." God implies that, by listening carefully to what the *angel* says, Israel will be doing what *God* says. Whatever originality and imagination angels may possess, they do not use those gifts to make up their own lines but only to express as effectively as they can what God wants them to say and do.

That brings us to the other important function of angels— at least one of significant interest to human beings. Do God's angels protect us?

Guardians of Believers

Mothers with small children often believe in guardian angels. One mother I talked to lived on a busy street. Her children were absolutely not allowed to cross that street unattended by an adult. One early evening she left her three-year-old son—we'll call him "Paul"—with his father while she went for a walk. She had crossed the busy street but was still quite close to home when she heard the noise of a Big Wheel tricycle on the sidewalk behind her. It was little Paul, grinning happily. He had evidently escaped the notice of his dad and crossed the busy street.

"Paul," she asked, trying to hide the fear in her voice, "how did you get across the street?"

"It was easy," he said, smiling. "I just closed my eyes and prayed for the angels to keep me safe."

Neither Paul nor his mother doubted that the angels had done just that.

A Clear Biblical Teaching

Sometimes when I'm speaking about angels to a church group, I will quote from memory, without giving the source, a version of Psalm 91:11-12: "For he will command his angels concerning you to guard you in all your ways; they will lift you up in their hands, so that you will not strike your foot against a stone." And if I then ask, "Who said that?" the first and usually prevailing answer is "the devil" or "Satan."

That answer is correct, of course. The devil did quote (misquote?) these words when he tempted Jesus to cast himself down from the pinnacle of the Temple (Matthew 4:6; Luke 4:10-11). This episode gives rise to the oft-quoted saying: "Even the devil knows how to quote Scripture."

However, it's more important to remember that the first person who said these words was the believer in Psalm 91 and that this passage has become the classic biblical support for the belief in guardian angels. These words about God's care through angels—as the little word "for" in verse 11 indicates—support the affirmations found in Psalm 91:9-10: "If you make the Most High your dwelling—even the LORD, who is my refuge—then no harm will befall you, no disaster will come near your tent."

Notice that the psalm says: "He will command his angels

concerning you" (v. 11). Thus God uses angels to protect the believer from harm and disaster. God provides *His* care for us *through* them.

Psalm 91 does not stand alone in its teaching. Psalm 34:7 says: "The angel of the LORD encamps around those who fear him, and he delivers them." In the early books of the Old Testament—Genesis through Judges—there is frequent reference to an "angel of the LORD" who provided security for God's people. Exodus 23:20: "See, I am sending an angel ahead of you to guard you along the way and to bring you to the place I have prepared." Two "men" or "angels" saved Lot and his family out of Sodom and Gomorrah (Genesis 19:1-22). The "angel of the LORD" protected Isaac at the time of God's testing of Abraham (22:9-18). Angels of God met Jacob on his way to meet with Esau and provided the sense of security that Jacob needed when he confessed: "This is the camp of God" (32:1-2).

And we certainly cannot bypass the story found in 2 Kings 6:8-23. When Elisha's servant awoke and saw the Aramean army with horses and chariots, he was understandably afraid. "Oh, my lord, what shall we do?" (v. 15) he asked Elijah. "'Don't be afraid,' the prophet answered. 'Those who are with us are more than those who are with them'" (v. 16). "Then the Lord opened the servant's eyes, . . . and he looked and saw the hills full of horses and chariots of fire all around Elisha" (v. 17). That is a truth meant to give security and comfort to God's people.

The New Testament also provides many examples of guardian angels. After His temptation in the wilderness, Jesus "was with the wild animals, and angels attended him" (Mark 1:13). Later, at Jesus' arrest, Peter, attempting to protect his master, drew his sword and cut off the ear of the high priest's servant. Jesus told him to put away his sword and said, "Do you think I cannot call on my Father, and he will at once put at my disposal more than twelve legions of angels?" (Matthew 26:53).

Jesus knew that God's angels were available for protection and security, not only for himself but also for God's little ones: "See that you do not look down on one of these little ones. For I tell you that their angels in heaven always see the face of my Father in heaven" (Matthew 18:10).

A Tough Question

About this point in one of my lectures on angels, some of my listeners are bound to raise an objection. They gladly admit that the Bible clearly teaches that there are guardian angels, but that raises a problem in their minds. What about Christians who are not spared from harm or disaster? What has happened to their guardian angels? Do guardian angels take days off?

At the heart of such questions is this core question: Why are some people kept from harm and danger while others are not, and how is that related to the function of angels as guardians?

On one level that is an easy question to answer, but on another level it is very difficult. The easy part relates to the function of guardian angels. Remember that when we looked at Psalm 91:11-12, we noted that guardian angels never act on their own. God is the One who commands His angels concerning believers. Angels, including guardian angels, only do what God tells them to do. So when we question why some little child of the Kingdom was not protected from harm, we ultimately are questioning the will of God.

Before we start asking about the will of God, let's face an often-heard objection to the answer that I just gave. I have contended throughout this study that angels never do anything on their own but only and always do God's will. Psalm 91:11-12 and other scriptures support that notion.

Many people are not satisfied with the idea that angels never act on their own. Perhaps that's because they think along the lines of today's business model. They picture a chief executive officer (God) who gives department managers (angels) quite a lot of leeway, as long as they (department managers/angels) get the job done.

Or maybe some dislike the Scriptures' teaching because they think that such complete obedience is boring—that it makes angels into some sort of celestial robots and doesn't allow them any creative input. Perhaps they are forgetting that in the new heaven and the new earth those who are saved will never again be able to do wrong. We will be able only and ever to do the will of God—just like the angels.

I personally do not find that prospect boring. And I don't think angels find it boring either.

But we must return to the question: If all things happen according to God's perfect will, why are some believers saved from disaster while others are not? This is a valid question, whether God works directly or through the agency of angels. However, on this side of heaven, it's a question that's very difficult to answer. We are often confronted with tragic accidents in the lives of believers and their children, and we ask the Lord over and over: Why? Why? Why?

I know of no easy answers. I do know that we as Christians have at the heart of our faith the cross of Jesus—a cross of suffering and even shame. God did not prevent that suffering from happening to the One of whom He said: "This is my Son, whom I love; with him I am well pleased" (2 Peter 1:17). So the tragedy of suffering somehow fits within the confines of God's love. We must never give up on that love—even when we suffer.

Special Angels for Children?

Earlier we looked at Jesus' words in Matthew 18:10: "See that you do not look down on one of these little ones. For I tell you that their angels in heaven always see the face of my Father in heaven." This verse often raises an interesting question: Is there a special contingent of guardian angels assigned to the care of the children of the Kingdom?

Traditionally that has been the understanding of this text.

Furthermore, as I indicated earlier in this chapter, mothers with small children somehow feel that there must be a specially caring and efficient company of angels in charge of the safety of their children. Children need such acute care.

The traditional interpretation may be correct. It is also possible, perhaps even more likely, that "these little ones" in verse 10 refers not so much to children as to believers who have humbled themselves as little children. That is the point Jesus makes earlier. "Unless you change and become like little children, you will never enter the kingdom of heaven" (v. 3). "Whoever humbles himself like this child is the greatest in the kingdom of heaven" (v. 4). The emphasis is upon adults who become trusting and unpretentious—like little children. In verse 5 the emphasis appears to be on welcoming one who is child*like,* and in verse 6 it seems almost certain that Jesus is referring to an adult believer who is like a little child: "If anyone causes one of these little ones who believe in me to sin." So the command in verse 10 probably also refers to an adult believer who has a childlike trust in Christ.

It seems likely then that Matthew 18:10 is referring to all believers who have childlike trust in Jesus. Of course, that does not exclude children. Children, after all, are the model of what childlike trust in Jesus really is. They also are under God's providential care through angels.

Are There Individual Guardian Angels?

Another question, frequently raised, is whether a specific angel is perpetually assigned to each individual believer. When the heavenly duty roster came out, was one specific angel assigned to your personal care and security?

Some people believe that Acts 12:1-19 teaches this. You remember the story: Peter had been cast into prison by Herod. The church was meeting at the home of the mother of John Mark, praying for Peter's release. Meanwhile, an "angel of the Lord" came and miraculously extricated Peter from prison (though Peter himself thought he was seeing a vision). Outside the prison, Peter became aware that an angel had rescued him from Herod's clutches. He went to the home of John Mark's mother and knocked at the outer entrance. Rhoda, the maid, came to answer the door and announced to the praying church that Peter was outside. The church found Rhoda's announcement hard to believe: "You're out of your mind," they said. When Rhoda kept on insisting, they said: "It must be *his* angel" (v. 15, emphasis added). Finally, Peter was allowed to enter and greet the astonished church.

Even though they were praying earnestly for Peter's release, they—like so many of us today—were still astonished to find their prayers answered in this positive fashion. Note that they said "*his* angel" (v. 15, emphasis added). This affirmation no doubt reflects the thinking of the Early Church gathered there. They believed that everyone had a personal guardian angel who might occasionally show himself in bodily form and who might resemble in appearance the person under his care.

So it is possible that there is a personal guardian angel assigned to each believer. On the other hand, this passage really only proves that some early Christians believed that to be the case. Since this passage is not supported by any other Scripture passages, it does not carry much weight in proving the existence of individually assigned guardian angels.

One reformer said that we should say only that which is "true, sure, and profitable" about angels. He raised the question of whether it is really "profitable" to believe in individually assigned guardian angels. He pointed out that, if I am not satisfied by the fact that the whole heavenly host is watching out for me, it is not clear what benefit I would derive from knowing that one angel has been assigned as my personal guardian.

Perhaps we have individually assigned angels; perhaps we don't. The critically important fact we must remember is that it is really *God's* care through the angel that gives us security. God is the One who loved us enough to have sent His

Son to die for us. This love finds its source in God, not in angels.

One final word. The biblical teaching on God's care through guardian angels is not meant to make us careless or irresponsible. Do you remember when the devil quoted Psalm 91:11-12 in the temptation of Jesus (Matthew 4:5-7; Luke 4:9-12)? He was encouraging Jesus to throw himself down from the pinnacle of the Temple. Jesus responded with another text from Scripture: "It is also written: 'Do not put the Lord your God to the test'" (Matthew 4:7).

Jesus' answer is a good one for us to keep in mind. God and His angels are not an insurance policy against all avoidable catastrophes that come into the human life. Our God-given good sense is often more important than any number of angels trying to overcome our bouts of foolishness.

Background Scripture: Genesis 19:1-22; 22:9-18; 31:1-2; Exodus 23:20-22; Deuteronomy 6:16; 1 Samuel 16:19; 2 Kings 6:8-23; Psalms 34:7; 91:9-12; Ecclesiastes 5:6; Haggai 1:13; Malachi 2:7; 3:1; Matthew 4:5-7; 11:10; 18:1-10; 26:53; Mark 1:2; Luke 4:9-12; 7:24; 7:27; 9:52; Acts 12:1-19; James 2:25; 2 Peter 1:17

This chapter is adapted from *In the Company of Angels,* by Andrew J. Bandstra, © 1995 by CRC Publications, 2850 Kalamazoo S.E., Grand Rapids, MI 49560. Copublished with Servant Publications, Ann Arbor, MI 48107. All rights reserved. Used by permission.

There is a classic painting that many parents of young children have framed and mounted on the walls of homes. It is a picture of a father kneeling beside the bed of his sleeping child, praying earnestly. At the top of the portrait, one can look out the window to this little child's room and see high in the night sky the representation of a good and of an evil spirit doing battle with each other, apparently vying for the vulnerable young soul. The caption at the bottom of the painting quotes Ephesians 6:12: "For our struggle is not against flesh and blood, but against the rulers, against the authorities, against the powers of this dark world and against the spiritual forces of evil in the heavenly realms." What is the nature of this heavenly battle? And what is the nature of the "powers of this dark world"?

CHAPTER 5

Satan and Demons

by Gene Van Note

DO YOU HAVE A PERSONAL DEMON? One who sits on your shoulder and whispers attractive temptations in your ear? One who slyly suggests ways you can beat the system without hurting anyone very much? One you can blame when your wrong choices become public?

Some people believe that demons are everywhere, perhaps even filling the air we breathe. Listen to this observation about life from one whose community considered him a wise man, "Every person is surrounded by demons, a thousand on the left and ten thousand on the right." Those words come from the Haggadah, the collection of ancient Jewish folklore. The legends insist that weakness in the knees is a sign that demons are present. Beyond that, the ancients thought that demons crowded spiritual leaders so tightly they wore out the garments of the leaders. When bruises appeared on anyone's feet, it was a sign that the demons had trampled on them.

According to the Haggadah, especially the teachings of Rabbi Huna, an ancient who wanted to see demons should follow these strange and grotesque instructions: Take the afterbirth of a black cat which is the firstborn of a litter from a black cat that was also the firstborn. Parch the afterbirth in a fire, grind it into powder, and put a generous pinch of the mix into each eye. Then that person can see the demons. Or so the old tales say.[1]

A observant person might suggest that if you put ashes in your eyes, you might not see anything but demons—for a long time!

But what does the Bible say?

Is it dangerous to sit under a drain pipe because the discharged water contains demons? Must a person not step outside the house on Wednesday and Saturday nights because on those nights the demons roam in the dark?

That's what the Haggadah says.

But what does the Bible say?

We suspect that the biblical message about demons and their master, Satan, is different from what we have just read; so let's turn to the Bible to discover what the Bible has to say about these representatives of evil.

Satan and His Hosts in the Old Testament

As I write this, the snap of fall is in the air and Halloween masks are in the stores. I saw a popular one the other day—a rubberized pull-over full-head mask of the devil, or at least our culture's idea of what the devil looks like. In a few days goblins and ghosts, devils and witches will walk the streets looking for candy from neighbors and friends. Make no mistake, though merchants may cleverly advertise that their "devilish" merchandise is for "ghouls and boys," the Bible takes a much more serious view of witches and demons. The biblical message is clear: Satan and his hosts are real and have been masters of deception and matters of concern for a long, long time.

Surprisingly, however, the Old Testament has little to say about demons and not much more about their master, Satan.

Satan made his first appearance very early in the salvation story as the serpent in Genesis 3 who tempted our first parents to sin. That tragic scene is referred to by the apostle Paul in 2 Corinthians 11:3. However, not in Genesis 3 nor anywhere else in the Old Testament is the serpent identified as Satan. It is John in Revelation 12:9 who writes, "That ancient serpent called the devil, or Satan . . . leads the whole world astray." Finally, we learn what had been suspected for a long time—the clever serpent was, in fact, Satan in disguise.

The noun translated "Satan" appears only six times in the Hebrew Bible. The Septuagint, the Greek translation of the Old Testament, uses the word *diabolos* where Satan appears in the Hebrew. Obviously that's the origin of our word "diabolical," which means "something characteristic of the devil." That gives us a clue to the primary meaning of the word, for *diabolos* identifies a person given to malicious gossip, a slanderer.

Satan is the one who defamed the character of Job (chapters 1 and 2), accused God's servant (Zechariah 3:1), and evilly influenced David to take a census of Israel (1 Chronicles 21:1). Satan was deeply involved with sin in the Old Testament without, however, any reference to him as an independent evil being ruling a demonic kingdom. In fact, there is no observable connection between demons and Satan in the Old Testament. The full development of that idea would come later.

Between Malachi and Matthew

The Jewish religious literature written in the 400-year intertestamental period (from Malachi to Matthew) has an increasing number of references to Satan and his demons. Opinions vary as scholars search for the reasons for the growth of Jewish teaching on the devil and demons. It may have resulted from their exposure to Persian religion and its Zoroastrian dualism while they were in captivity in Babylon. The Zoroastrians taught that good and evil are competing forces of equal strength fighting for control of the world.

Jewish teaching concerning Satan and his hosts did not form the basis of Jesus' teaching nor create the continual hostility between Jesus and demons in the Gospels. It does, however, help us understand confrontation between good and evil as the common folk in Jesus' day might have understood it.

The Gospels

We see Jesus through the lens of 2,000 years of Christian history and the diligent study of hundreds of scholars throughout the generations. We see Him at the Resurrection, the Ascension, and Pentecost through the pages of the Holy Bible.

However, those who played with Him as a boy and walked with Him as a man did not have the benefit of the knowledge of the empty Tomb or the power of the Holy Spirit who guides to all wisdom. They saw Him as an average person with nothing that set Him off from the crowd. Think about the day He waited to be baptized by John in the Jordan River. The crowd focused their attention on John, not on Jesus. He was just one more person in the line.

To these first-century onlookers, it would have been quite obvious that a major shift in the life of Jesus happened after He began His formal ministry. Whereas, before, Jesus was one of the crowd, afterward it is clear that the forces of good and evil were doing battle and His life and person were the battleground.

Mark tells us that "immediately [following His baptism] the Spirit *impelled* Him [Jesus] to go out into the wilderness" (1:12, NASB, emphasis added). The word "impelled" is the same word used in Mark 1:34, 39 when Jesus cast out demons. In the Greek the word has a broad range of meanings from which the translator can choose: from "impelled" (NASB) to "sent . . . out" (NIV). Whether you conclude the word means "expel" or "nudge out gently," one thing is clear—God did not fear or back away from the confrontation with the devil. That fact has enormous implications that we will explore in the next chapter.

Nor did the powers of darkness leave Jesus alone after He had rejected the devil's shortcuts to victory. In fact, according to Mark's Gospel, Jesus had barely completed calling the first disciples when a man "possessed by an evil spirit" identified Jesus in the synagogue in Capernaum (1:23-27).

Let's look at a brief sampling of the encounters with the demonic forces that served, to some extent at least, to define Jesus' ministry. The New Testament takes for granted the existence of Satan and demons. It is important to note that in the Greek New Testament the devil is never called a "demon" nor are demons called "devils."

The healing ministry of Jesus included release from all kinds of demon possession. On some occasions the demons knew Jesus' identity, such as the one in the synagogue just referred to and the legion of demons who inhabited the man who lived in the tombs across the lake in the region of the Gerasenes (Mark 1:23-26 and 5:1-20). At other times Jesus released people from physical or emotional suffering caused by demons (Matthew 9:32-34 and 17:14-18, for example).

Satan is seen in the New Testament as an independent evil power, a supernatural adversary of God who cleverly tempts Christian believers and led Judas to betray Christ (1 Timothy 3:7; John 13:2, 27). He is a murderer and a liar who is disguised as an angel of light, who keeps the gospel from unbelievers, exercises control over them, and has the power of death over those outside the church (John 8:44; 2 Corinthians 11:14; Luke 8:12; Colossians 1:13; Hebrews 2:14). And that's just the *short* list of Satan's dark power over humanity in his violent opposition to the One who said of himself, "I am the light of the world" (John 8:12).

The New Testament Beyond the Gospels

Outside the Gospels, neither Satan nor demons are mentioned very often in the rest of the New Testament. However, their existence is taken for granted without any suggestion that their power has been diminished.

The first recorded incident involving the devil, beyond the Gospel accounts, comes early in Acts where Peter speaks words to Ananias that are hard to hear but easy to understand, "Why has Satan filled your heart to lie to the Holy Spirit?" (5:3, NASB). New Testament scholars continue to debate the meaning of the final New Testament reference to the devil, "When the thousand years are over, Satan will be released from his prison" (Revelation 20:7). In between these New Testament books, various terms are used to highlight different aspects of the evil abilities of God's adversary.

Philo Judaeus, also known as Philo of Alexandria, fairly represents the ideas of a majority of Jews and Greeks in New Testament times. Living from 20 B.C. to A.D. 50, he combined both Jewish and Greek philosophy by believing that there were spirits flying everywhere through the air. To Philo, the air was full of disembodied spirits. Like Philo, the people of the New Testament age, both Jews and Greeks, believed that the air was filled with spirits, some good, mostly bad. And anyone who breathed the air was a potential victim or benefactor of these airborne spirits.

The apostle Paul, trained in both Jewish and Greek schools, firmly believed that Christians were being assaulted by the spirits of evil. To the Corinthians he wrote, "*The god of this age* has blinded the minds of unbelievers, so that they cannot see the light of the gospel of the glory of Christ, who is the image of God" (2 Corinthians 4:4, emphasis added). Writing to the Ephesians, he enlarged on this idea saying, "The ruler of the kingdom of the air . . . is now at work in those who are disobedient" (2:2). Then he added, "Our struggle is not against flesh and blood, but against . . . the powers of this dark world and against the spiritual forces of evil in the heavenly realms" (6:12). We'll see in the next chapter how Paul felt this battle would end, but here it is enough to note that the apostle was convinced there was an evil power present in this world.

Peter, James, and John concur, each saying words similar to these in 1 Peter 5:8, "Your enemy the devil prowls around like a roaring lion looking for someone to devour" (see also James 4:7 and 1 John 5:18). At times, and in some places, the devil was believed to have great power. John wrote to the church at Pergamum, "I know where you live—where Satan has his throne" (Revelation 2:13). To warn his Christian friends, John wrote about "that ancient serpent called the devil, or Satan, who leads the whole world astray" (12:9). The Early Church had no doubt. They were engaged in a vigorous and violent battle with a personal adversary who was totally evil and intended to drag everyone down with him, if he could. And he tried!

That Was Then and This Is Now

Nearly 2,000 years have passed since John wrote about the final battle between God and Satan. We have neither time nor space to make more than two or three stopovers in history from the "then" to the "now."

Martin Luther, key leader of the Protestant Reformation, wrote "A Mighty Fortress Is Our God" in 1529. In it he expressed his concern about the presence and power of a personal devil with these words:

> *For still our ancient foe*
> *Doth seek to work us woe;*
> *His craft and power are great,*
> *And armed with cruel hate,*
> *On earth is not his equal.*

John Wesley, our spiritual pioneer who lived in the 18th century, is said to have literally thrown an inkwell at the devil who, Wesley believed, was harassing him in his study one day.

Ootah, the native American who accompanied Robert Peary to the North Pole in 1910, said, "The devil is asleep or having trouble with his wife, or we should never have come back so easily."[2]

Of course, people today are too sophisticated to believe all that traditional stuff. We live in a scientific age. We're not the kind of people you see in the pages of the *National Geographic* involved in strange rituals to control evil spirits. It figures that since the modern mind says you can't see God at the end of a telescope, it would also say you won't be able to see the devil there either. Modern science is not friendly to any idea that cannot be proven. Except, of course, their solid belief in the constituent parts of the atom, which have never been seen but are widely accepted as existing—but that's another story.

Scientists are not alone in disputing or discarding the idea of Satan. Some leaders among the clergy have voiced their agreement: "If you try to have one satanic character representing all the universe's malevolence, people today just don't buy it," said one pastor in the Midwest. "It doesn't resonate with their experience. For most of us, evil is more ineffable and elusive than that," he added.[3]

On the other hand, the entertainment industry seems to have fallen in love with Satan and his demons or, in some cases, with God and His angels. To be sure, movies about the devil and God take us to the edge of the absurd—perhaps beyond. However, there have been a great many movies and countless television dramas about the devil. *Leonard Maltin's Movie and Video Guide* lists 61 films that begin with the word "Devil" and 10 that begin with "Satan." But that doesn't come close to a complete list and doesn't include films that do not have Satan in the title but are focused on him, such as *Rosemary's Baby* (released in 1968) and *The Exorcist* (1973).

However, even though the scientific approach rejects the notion of a personal devil and some religious leaders conclude that the idea doesn't "resonate with experience," the devil has many believers around the world. Voodoo cults throughout the Caribbean are an example of the presence of satanic worship in the late 20th century. These cults, reshaped, are appearing in the United States in a worship form known as Santeria.

Still, it's not necessary to go to primitive forms of worship to find allegiance to Satan. You can see it on the T-shirts teenagers wear to high school. Now, to be sure, teens rarely pass up a chance to tweak the noses or feed the fears of their parents' generation. It is not easy to distinguish between a sincerely-held belief and an opportunity to win a skirmish in the battle of the generations. Whatever the motivation, on the basis of freedom of religion, young people have won the right in the United States to wear satanic T-shirts in public as an expression of their "religious" faith.

However, there is no question about the intensity of devotion to satanic causes when devil-worshipers kill a pet as part of their worship before killing classmates at school. That type of incident happened recently in Mississippi when a young man stabbed his mother to death before going to high school with a rifle under his coat. There he killed two girls and wounded seven others as part of a murder conspiracy hatched by the small group of teenage Satanists. The killer said, "That murder was a viable means of accomplishing the purpose and goals of [their] shared belief system."[4]

On the other hand, a wide variety of Christian believers, representing both traditional and contemporary forms of theology and worship, share some kind of belief in demons, demon possession, or demonism as some would prefer to call it. Some groups are controlled by rigid rules and regulations in both the recognition and exorcism of demons. In those religious communities, such work is the exclusive province of experts trained in that specialty. Other groups allow nearly anyone "with the gift" to identify demon possession and command the evil intruder to leave.

Many, perhaps the majority, of believers in all branches and expressions of Christianity are reluctant to claim either the ability to identify or the power to exorcise demons from the one demonized. In chapter 6, we'll visit with a missionary who spent many years in Haiti. He will give us some clues on how to distinguish evil spirits and some appropriate responses.

Though, as Martin Luther's hymn asserts, on earth the devil has no equal, he does have limits. We'll explore what those are and the assuring message to Christians in the next chapter.

---

1. All references to Jewish folklore come from *The Book of Legends,* edited by Hayim Nahman Bialik and Yehoushua Hana Ravnitsky, translated by William G. Braude (New York: Shocken Books, 1992), 793.

2. Emily Morrison Beck, ed., *John Bartlett's Familiar Quotations* (Boston: Little, Brown and Company, 1980), 679.

3. "The Devil Next Door," *Kansas City Star,* November 1, 1997, E-1.

4. *Kansas City Star,* October 17, 1997, A-8.

Background Scripture: Genesis 3; 1 Chronicles 21:1; Job 1—2; Zechariah 3:1; Matthew 9:32-34; 17:14-18; Mark 1:12, 23-27, 34, 39; 5:1-20; Luke 8:12; John 8:12, 44; 12:2; 13:27; Acts 5:3; 2 Corinthians 4:4; 11:3, 14; Ephesians 2:2; 6:12; Colossians 1:13; 1 Timothy 3:7; Hebrews 2:14; James 4:7; 1 Peter 5:8; 1 John 5:18; Revelation 2:13; 12:9; 20:6

About the Author: Rev. Gene Van Note is the former executive editor of Sunday School curriculum for the Church of the Nazarene. Gene is now retired and lives in Overland Park, Kansas.

In recent years, a series of novels by Christian writer Frank Peretti, beginning with his acclaimed *This Present Darkness,* brought the imagery of spiritual warfare to the forefront of Christian discussion. His novels pitted a very real devil involved in very real battle against unsuspecting and unprepared churches and Christians. His novels were hailed by some as a wake-up call to the power of Satan and his evil influence in all parts of our daily lives. Others thought Peretti had gone too far and had Christians cowering in fear of a demon under every bed and behind every door. What is an appropriate view of Satan? Is he best described as a wild-eyed, long-fanged, blood-dripping ghoul? Or does a profile of Satan go far beyond mere physical attributes? In either case, what defense do Christians have against such a fierce foe?

CHAPTER 6

Spiritual Warfare and Armor Too

by Gene Van Note

IN EARLY MAY 1866, the United States District Court of Virginia handed down an indictment accusing Jefferson Davis of treason against the federal government. That indictment read in part, "Jefferson Davis not having fear of God before his eyes . . . but being moved and seduced by the devil . . . to subvert and to stir, move and incite insurrection, rebellion and war . . ."[1]

The charge of treason against the former president of the Confederate States of America is not the primary focus of this chapter. Yet, we should note in passing that Davis was released on a writ of habeas corpus on May 10, 1867, and never brought to trial.

What is important to us at this point is that, at one time in history, a United States federal court issued an indictment including the words "seduced by the devil." What happened to the hallowed doctrine of the separation of church and state in the United States? Perhaps that was before it was rediscovered in the Constitution. At the very least, it shows how much people are affected by the culture that surrounds them.

That should come as no surprise. People have always been molded by their culture. The Jewish rabbinic traditions, which had great influence in Jesus' time, insisted that Satan was far more active in ancient history than the Old Testament directly reveals. The traditions taught that, in addition to his escapade in the Garden and his part in the testing of Job, Satan was responsible for many of the sins mentioned in their Bible—such as the Israelites worshiping the golden calf at Sinai and David's sin with Bathsheba. Satan also, according to those widely held traditions, provoked non-Jews to ridicule Jewish laws, thus weakening the religious loyalties of the Jews.

Jesus Was a Man of His Times

Jesus is a man of all times and every age and generation. Yet, as the incarnate Son of God, He lived at a specific time in history. When Paul wrote in Philippians 2:7 that Jesus was "made in human likeness," he affirmed that Jesus took on the limitations of time and space common to all of us. Jesus was born into a culture with beliefs and prejudices, habits and customs.

Without a doubt, that culture not only believed in the devil and demons but experienced their destructive power as well. Yet, while the demons of the New Testament could generate great fear, they were not considered so uncommon that people put them in a carnival tent and charged admission to see them at work. Or it may be that people were too afraid of that kind of contact with or attempted control of demons. We know of one occasion when the owners of a possessed girl used her to earn money for them by her ability to predict the future (Acts 16:16-18). There was a common cultural understanding about the devil and his demons against which the battle between Jesus and the forces of darkness was played out.

Who was Jesus as revealed by His interaction with the demons? If it is true, at least to some extent, that Jesus' ministry was defined to his generation by the actions of the devil and his demons, then we need to ask what their hostility revealed.

The record of conflict between the Light of the World and the forces of darkness is not complicated, though parts of it are hidden in the mists of history and the mystery of the occult. Let's take a quick look at the gospel story in this regard. Four things stand out:

- Demons are powerful and often opposed Jesus.
- They knew who He was.
- They recognized His authority over them and obeyed His commands.
- These confrontations revealed Jesus as a truly remarkable person, one who had the power of God in Him.

No New Testament passage about demons contains all four aspects mentioned above. Perhaps the one that comes closest is Luke 4:31-37. Though not a complete picture, it gives us some breadth of understanding, so let's begin there.

One day the devout in Capernaum asked Jesus to teach in the synagogue. A very normal scene—until it was interrupted by an evil spirit inhabiting a man. The evil spirit immediately recognized Jesus and cried out, "I know who you are—the Holy One of God!" (v. 34). Throughout the gospel story, often Jesus was first recognized by demons (see also Mark 1:23-24; 5:1-20).

The pattern of Jesus' power over the demons was clearly demonstrated in the synagogue that day in Capernaum when Jesus said, "'Be quiet! . . . Come out of him!' Then the demon threw the man down before them all and came out without injuring him" (Luke 4:35).

The result was predictable, forming a pattern followed to one extent or another throughout the Gospels. "All the people were amazed and said to each other, 'What is this teaching? With authority and power he gives orders to evil spirits and they come out!'" (v. 36).

Who was Jesus as defined by His own words and actions? One day, after He had become at least a minor celebrity, Jesus went home to Nazareth (vv. 16-28). That can be risky. It was for Jesus. His boyhood friends became so angry because of what He said in the synagogue they tried to murder Him. He made them mad when He read from Isaiah and then said, "Today this scripture is fulfilled in your hearing" (v. 21).

What scripture? These words from Isaiah 61:1-2: "The Spirit of the Sovereign LORD is on me, because the LORD has anointed me to preach good news to the poor. He has sent me to bind up the brokenhearted, to proclaim freedom for the captives and release from darkness for the prisoners, to proclaim the year of the LORD's favor."

Our focus is not on their anger but on the Old Testament passage Jesus chose to define His life and work. Note that when Jesus pictured himself and what He was about, He did not say a specific word about casting out demons; yet He did not hesitate to do battle with them. His emphasis was on freedom, healing, and salvation—not just to the privileged but to the poor as well. Clearly He was fulfilling the prophetic word of the angel to Joseph, "You are to give him the name Jesus, because *he will save his people from their sins*" (Matthew 1:21, emphasis added).

Jesus confirmed the angel's promise when He said, "The Son of Man came to seek out and to save the lost" (Luke 19:10, NRSV). Jesus was not obsessed with the representatives of darkness. He didn't begin each morning as if it were a hunting expedition for demons. Nor did He say to His disciples at breakfast, "Go find a demon-possessed person today so I can impress the crowd." When the demons tried to identify Jesus' true nature, He often ordered them to be silent and tell no one who He was (Luke 4:41, for example). Jesus was not concerned with His reputation as a demon destroyer. His concern was always for these unfortunate people, a love that was part of His larger goal to redeem the world.

Sooner or later we want to know what all that means to us who are living after two millennia of the Christian era. So let's explore that a bit.

What About Demonic Activity Today?

There are 75 references to demons, evil spirits, and the devil in the four Gospels. The remaining 23 books of the New Testament contain only 28 references to the devil and his hosts—about one-third of the Gospel total. The problem didn't disappear, but the intensity and frequency of the opposition did. Or more probably, the devil took a different approach from the frontal attack he used on Jesus.

Satanic activity, demonism, and a fascination with the occult has ebbed and flowed like the tide across the centuries. We seem to be in a period of considerable interest in forces that cannot be explained by scientific formulas, and the curiosity is worldwide. Note these brief examples:

Recently a secretary in an Italian city near Naples was asked by a stranger to tamper with the voter registration lists. She refused. A few days later, she became ill, unable to eat or sleep. Specialists in Naples and Rome could find no physical problem. Finally, in desperation, her family took her to Annamaria Ammendola, a local magician who specializes in casting out demons and evil spirits. The news report said, "She [Annamaria] gathered up her cosmic energy—a process that takes two or three days of intense concentration—and then broke the spell and restored the clerk to health." The incredible thing is that no one in the community thought it remarkable. Italians are cosmopolitan and well-educated, yet there are an estimated 20,000 to 30,000 magicians earning a total of about $20 million yearly in Italy.[2]

We, of course, have no time or interest in such hocus-pocus. Or do we? Papa George advertises on the Internet that he can customize voodoo spells for each of his clients. "The difference between psychics and voodoo," says Papa George, "is that psychics predict and voodoo gets results. I make people want what you want them to want. Everything in life comes down to influence—between God and the devil." Then he adds, "If this ad upsets you, I am sorry, but we have freedom of speech. If you have a problem with this, move to China. And remember that for everyone this ad upsets, there are 10 people who want to read it!"

Perhaps, perhaps not.

However, public interaction with the devil and his agents is not popular among most people in North America. We like our paganism in more subtle doses. By contrast, in many places in our world the conflict is open and brutal.

Some time ago a Haitian ferry boat sank en route from the island of Gonaive to the mainland, taking about 200 people to their deaths. Haitians on Gonaive accused the owner of a rival ferry of using voodoo to cause the boat to sink. So they burned his boat and tried to lynch his wife, who was rescued by the local police.[3]

A Report from the Front Lines

One of the blessings and burdens of having been a missionary to Haiti is that people often ask, "You don't really believe in demons and possession do you?" At least that has been the experience of Dr. Paul Orjala (pronounced or-e-AH-lah) who, with his wife, Mary, served the Lord and the church in Haiti for more than 15 years.

Orjala's depth of experience and personal contact with voodoo and demon possession provides a unique insight to demonism. When the Orjalas went to Haiti in 1950, they were among the first evangelical missionaries in that island country. On many occasions they observed satanic power as people were taken over by demonic forces. The Haitians use the picture of a horse and rider to describe what happens in possession. The person is the "horse," the pagan god—Satan's agent—mounts the saddle and then "rides."

"Haiti is 90 percent Catholic but 100 percent voodoo" was a common Haitian proverb when the Orjalas arrived in Port au Prince, the national capitol. Orjala writes, "Our Haitian Christians believe that the real power of voodoo is of satanic origin, and I agree with them. Satan works in different ways in different cultures, but always his aim is the same—to alienate people from God."[4]

Paul Orjala summarizes demonic activity in these three categories:

- *Oppression:* physical or psychological sickness imposed from a satanic origin (see Luke 13:11, 16).
- *Obsession:* fascination with demonic/satanic activity to

the point of giving oneself over to its service (see 1
Timothy 4:1; Revelation 9:20-21).
- *Possession:* subject to the will of an evil spirit.[5]

So the question arises: How can we tell the difference between physical or mental illness and demonic possession? Orjala begins with this caution, "Even in the Third World where
demon possession is taken for granted, it is a relatively rare
thing, and one should not be hasty in attributing disorders to
the work of evil spirits. One must carefully distinguish demon
possession from symptoms of sickness, neurosis or psychosis,
hysteria, hypnosis, exhibition, or expected cultural expression."[6]

Then he adds, "One may cautiously suspect demonic
possession when other normal explanations for the combined
symptoms are not adequate. Here is a summary from my own
observation and that of others:

- *Behavioral symptoms:* may include unusual strength,
  convulsions, aggressive or violent behavior, or catatonic
  withdrawal, sometimes accompanied by speaking in an
  unknown or unlearned language.
- *Psychological symptoms:* obvious inner conflict, sudden
  personality or emotional changes, depression, defiance,
  and clairvoyance (knowledge not naturally available).
- *Spiritual symptoms:* may include resistance to the things of
  God, reaction to or fear of the name of Jesus, blasphemy,
  recognition, and opposition to mature Christians. Symptoms may be affected by prayer causing either calm or
  more excitement."[7]

What's a Person to Do?

Does all this sound frightening? Of course. At least it
should. Daniel Williams writes, "The demons have power;
that is why they are feared. They can only be defeated by
power; that is why they must be exorcized."[8] Orjala adds this
encouraging word, "Sudden deliverance is possible through
divine help."

But we do not live in Haiti. Obviously our fight with the devil is going to be different. We'll not likely see many devil-worshipers and demon-possessed people. Only a very few of us will ever witness an exorcism. Dr. Orjala recognizes this when we allow him to complete this thought he began earlier in this chapter, "Satan works in different ways in different cultures but always his aim is the same—to alienate people from God." Then he added, "In sophisticated societies where science has largely replaced God, the idea of the supernatural—whether good or evil—has already been rejected for the most part. Why should Satan risk resurrecting the concept by manifesting his evil power [especially in the form of demon-possessed people] in such a society?"[9]

This brings us back to the words of the apostle Paul who, writing to the Ephesians, said, "Our struggle is not against enemies of blood and flesh, but . . . against the cosmic powers of this present darkness" (6:12, NRSV). Our battle is spiritual, not physical. It is to be fought against the powers of darkness.

This fight against evil does not reside in a formula. The temptation is to find an exorcism (a "magic" combination of words) that chases the devil and darkness away. But Paul said, "Be made powerful constantly in the Lord." That's the literal translation of Ephesians 6:10. This power does not come from human resources or external formulas. It is "in the Lord." When Christians live in union with Christ, in the orbit of His will, there cannot be failure due to powerlessness.

A few years ago we had an "October surprise," a very wet and thus an extremely heavy snowstorm. It caused extensive damage across our metro area. Major sections of the city were without electrical power. That, however, is not a picture of the power available for Christians. Believers are "being made powerful constantly as they are in the Lord." As long as they are "in Christ," that power cannot be cut off by external forces.

Hear again this promise as it is rendered in one paraphrase:

> Last of all I want to remind you that your strength

must come from the Lord's mighty power within you. Put on all of God's armor so that you will be able to stand safe against all strategies and tricks of Satan. For we are not fighting against people made of flesh and blood, but against persons without bodies—the evil rulers of the unseen world, those mighty satanic beings and great evil princes of darkness who rule this world; and against huge numbers of wicked spirits in the spirit world.

So use every piece of God's armor to resist the enemy whenever he attacks, and when it is all over, you will be standing up.

But to do this, you will need the strong belt of truth and the breastplate of God's approval. Wear shoes that are able to speed you on as you preach the Good News of peace with God. In every battle you will need faith as your shield to stop the fiery arrows aimed at you by Satan. And you will need the helmet of salvation and the sword of the Spirit—which is the Word of God.

Pray all the time. Ask God for anything in line with the Holy Spirit's wishes. Plead with Him, reminding Him of your needs, and keep praying earnestly for all Christians everywhere (*Ephesians 6:10-18*, TLB).

We come to the end of this stage of our journey, comforted and assured by the biblical picture of the power of God over Satan and his host. Nowhere does the Bible support the idea of dualism—the equality of good and evil forces in the universe. Rather, the Bible clearly affirms that good and evil are not equal. Whatever it may seem at specific times and places in history, evil was conquered on the Cross, a victory confirmed by the Resurrection.

As so we pray with our Master, "For thine is the Kingdom, and the power, and the glory forever, Amen."

---

1. Shelby Foote, *The Civil War: A Narrative* (New York: Vintage Books, 1974), vol. 3, 1036.

2. *Kansas City Star,* June 6, 1997, A-22.

3. *Kansas City Star,* September 12, 1997, A-5.

4. Paul Orjala, *This Is Haiti* (Kansas City: Nazarene Publishing House, 1961), 70.

5. *Emphasis,* June, July, August 1982, 21.

6. Ibid.

7. Ibid.

8. Daniel Day Williams, *The Demonic and the Divine* (Minneapolis: Fortress Press, 1990), 15.

9. Orjala, *This Is Haiti,* 70.

Background Scripture: Isaiah 61:1-2; Matthew 1:21; Mark 1:23; 5:1-20; Luke 4:16-18, 31-37, 41; 13:11-16; 19:10; Acts 16:16-18; Ephesians 2:12; 6:10-18; Philippians 2:7; 1 Timothy 4:1; Revelation 9:20-21

About the Author: Rev. Gene Van Note is the former executive editor of Sunday School curriculum for the Church of the Nazarene. Gene is now retired and lives in Overland Park, Kansas.

I have on my bookshelf a book with the title *Pagans and Christians* with the incredibly long subtitle *Religion and the Religious Life from the Second to the Fourth Century* A.D. *When the Gods of Olympus Lost Their Dominion and Christianity, with the Conversion of Constantine, Triumphed in the Mediterranean World.* Generally, when the word "pagan" is used, it refers to a time and culture in the dim past. Yet, for reasons not completely known, a revival of paganism in all its godless forms has catapulted into the culture of the 3rd millennium. The term "pagan" has again become a part of our modern vocabulary. Once more, "pagans and Christians" find themselves in the same arena as they did almost 3,000 years ago.

CHAPTER 7

Neopaganism: An Old Problem Reincarnated

by Joseph E. Coleson

GODDESS WORSHIP. Satanism. The occult. Astrology. Drug-based spirituality. Sophia. Horoscopes. Black cats. Summer solstice. White witches. Palm reading. Gaea. Shamanism. Formally, these are related to each other in different ways, but they and a host of other phenomena *are* related. They do share a common, non-Christian theological base, either in their essence or in the ways pagan systems use them.

The goal of this chapter is not to simply dismiss these pagan practices as non-Christian and move on past them. Because these systems of belief have infiltrated virtually every strata of society, we want to provide a brief introduction to the theology and practices of some of the common expressions of neopaganism ("new" or "revival of") found in North America today. This is not meant to scare or shock us; in Christ we are safe from all attacks, spells, or other harm some may wish to invoke upon us. The forces of darkness cannot do real harm to the child of God. But an informed Christian is one who is better able to both defend against and attack the ageless lies of the definition of paganism itself, Satan.

The underlying theological belief of the pagan systems we are considering in this chapter, and the one that ties them all together conceptually, is the belief that the creation itself—sun, moon, stars, and all that is on the earth—is god or a series of gods. In both the ancient and new paganism, nature is deified and worshiped.

Of course, human beings are part of nature too, so in this belief system—or set of belief systems—humans, too, are considered already or potentially divine. But we will leave for consideration in the next chapter those beliefs and systems— today grouped together under the term "New Age"—which assert that we humans are god, that god or deity is within us and must be encouraged to grow. In this chapter, we examine some of the expressions of the belief that nature is god or that God is only nature.

Divination—Arrows, Cards, Livers, and Runes

A common feature of many ancient and neopagan systems is the practice of divination. Divination of any kind— and there are many different varieties—is based on the belief that the gods reveal the future to those who will learn to read it. Reading the livers of sacrificial sheep, observing the flights of arrows, reading the pattern made by arrows dumped on the ground from a quiver, reading the pattern of a drop of oil on the surface of a bowl of water—all are examples of ancient Near Eastern divination.

All the ancient methods of divination required specialized training, passed on as part of the education of priests in the ancient religions. Reading of the livers of sacrificial sheep (technically called *hepatoscopy* [heh-pah-TAHS-cah-pee]) was the most common and important kind of divination in ancient Mesopotamia. It has left its record in thousands of clay models of sheep livers, models covered with written texts of instruction in how to read all the "liver" variations that could be found when a sheep was offered in the morning sacrifices.

Common modern examples of divination are the reading of Tarot cards, the reading of runes (mystery alphabets), palm reading, tea-leaf reading, and crystal-ball gazing. These and all the other forms of divination require specialized knowledge to interpret what is there to be read. In modern divination, as in ancient, the operative belief is that the gods or the spirits have revealed the future in these phenomena, available to any who will learn to read it there.

It is important to keep in mind that divination is not an attempt to control, influence, or change the future. Divination attempts only to *reveal* the future. Of course, the one for whom the reading is done then can take appropriate action. If good things are predicted, one can position oneself to be where they happen or make oneself ready to take advantage of them. If bad things are predicted, one can take measures to avoid them or to minimize their harmful impact. Still, divination, in and of itself, is not an attempt to control the future, only to predict it.

Magic—Spells, Curses, Amulets, and Dolls

Magic, by contrast, is the group of arts that promise to *control* the future. One aspect of that control is deterrence of specific dreaded events. This can involve protection from danger by the use of spells, amulets (ornamental charms), and so forth. Ezekiel 13:17-23 is a judgment against women who practiced both divination and magic. Their magic consisted of amulets worn on the wrist or on the head for the purpose of preserving their wearers from harm and/or of causing harm to those they wished to destroy.

This reminds us that magic also can be used to bring harm to one's enemies by spells, curses, or the destruction of dolls or other figures representing the enemy. When a practitioner sticks pins in a "voodoo doll," he or she believes that harm, or even death, will come to the person represented by the doll, the one that practitioner has been hired to harm or destroy. This and other practices are called "sympathetic magic." The person cursed is to receive, in reality, the destruction visited upon the figurine that stands for that person in the magical ritual.

In societies where belief in sympathetic magic is widespread, the intended targets also may believe in the powers of the practitioner. If they learn of the ritual curse, they often will sicken or even die. Whether this is due to the power of suggestion or whether demonic forces really do the bidding of the black magic practitioner—witch, shaman, medicine man or woman, or other—has been debated vigorously.

The ancients also practiced this form of magic. A group of figurines was found in an Egyptian archaeological context. Each figurine was inscribed with the name of an enemy city and/or its king, along with a curse calling for the destruction of that city and that king. Each figurine then was smashed so the curse upon city and king would be brought to pass. Such curses are called "execrations," so these figurines with their inscriptions are called the Egyptian Execration Texts. They are quite famous among ancient history buffs.

Goddess Worship

The archaeology of eastern Europe and western Asia indicates that goddess worship is the oldest form of paganism. Crudely shaped ceramic goddess figurines are the oldest religious objects found in archaeological contexts. The figurines attest to the belief that the mother earth goddess was responsible for human female fertility.

Recent scholarship suggests that some of the goddess figurines were used also for divination. Figurines used for this purpose were over-fired in a furnace deliberately so they would crack. The pattern of the cracking in the figurine determined the message, which would have been interpreted by cult personnel, probably the priestesses of the earth goddess.

Both the Old and New Testaments record the popularity of goddess worship. Israel and Judah, when they were unfaithful to God, worshiped Ishtar, the "queen of heaven," and Ashtoreth, the Canaanite manifestation of the earth goddess. In New Testament times, the earth goddess was worshiped in Asia Minor as Diana (her Roman name), Artemis (her Greek name), or Cybele (her ancient Anatolian name). Her temple at Ephesus was one of the seven wonders of the ancient world.

The silversmiths who made figurines of her for religious pilgrims started a disturbance in Ephesus against Paul when their revenues were threatened because so many people were becoming Christians (Acts 19:23-28).

Modern goddess worship includes worship of the mother earth goddess also. She still is regarded as responsible for fertility, but just as important is her shaping of a gentler, kinder (more "feminine") spirit in her worshipers toward the earth and all its children, including fellow human beings. Her name today is likely to be Gaea (JEE-a). Not everyone whose car carries the bumper sticker "Honor your mother" is a worshiper of the earth goddess, but some would be.

Another goddess is Sophia (soh-FEE-a); the name means "wisdom." A few people in some Christian denominations have attempted to set Sophia up as a feminine manifestation of God or as the fourth, female member of the godhead. They cite the statements of Proverbs that God created the world by wisdom (e.g., 3:19-20). The Septuagint (the first translation of the Hebrew Bible into Greek in the third century B.C.) translates the Hebrew word "wisdom" as "Sophia," which is the Greek word for "wisdom" (common noun) as well as the name of the goddess (proper noun). This is interpreted by some as giving biblical support to worship of Sophia.

Astrology

Astrology* is another ancient paganism that continues to be very popular in the modern world. In briefest terms, astrology is the belief that the stars, planets, and other heavenly bodies control (or greatly influence) human destiny. Therefore, human decisions should be made in accordance with their positions and alignments. That is why an astrologer asks the moment of a client's birth before giving a reading. This tells the astrologer the zodiacal sign one was born under, including the relative positions and ascendance or descendance of the moon and the planets at that moment. Those are the crucial factors in astrological thinking and determine the opportunities one should seize, as well as the risks and dangers one should avoid.

Shamanism

Shamanism is the practice of secret learning, the acquisition and use of esoteric (not widely known) knowledge, especially in the areas of spiritual knowledge available only to initiates. It includes the contact with the spirit world and "medical" practices that often combine herbal medicine with magical healing arts aimed at driving out demons or evil spirits. A shaman (SHAW-man or SHAY-man) can be either a man or a woman. The stereotypical "witch doctors" of some missionary stories were shamans. Shamanism was a feature of the ancient Celtic Druid religion, of certain eastern European and central Asian religions, of some Native American faiths, and continues in some New Age and occult belief systems. In ancient goddess worship, the priestesses often exercised the role of the shaman. Then, and in some modern goddess worship systems, the crone—a wise old woman in "the third stage of life"—was, among other things, a shaman.

Halloween, Solstices, and Other So-called Harmless Celebrations

Many special days on the calendar have their origins in ancient paganism. Whether their modern observance is pagan or not depends on a number of factors. The winter solstice was celebrated in northern Europe as the day when the light began once again to overcome the darkness, when the extremely short daylight hours of winter began to lengthen toward the spring.

The summer solstice was considered to be a time of special ability to contact the spirits, sprites, fairies, and other "little people." It was a time when good magic might happen but also when extra caution was needed to avoid trouble.

Halloween was the night that belonged to the departed

spirits. Halloween costumes originated in the belief that any ill-disposed spirit could be fooled into thinking the costumed person was not the one the spirit was looking for, and thus would not harm that person. Belief in the increased activity of witches on Halloween probably was linked with the movement of the departed spirits on that night.

Drug Use as a Spiritual Experience

Drugs have been used since prehistoric times. A cache of pipes and related items that well may have been used for drugs was found above the Dead Sea. They date to about 3500 B.C. Residue of opiates from poppy seeds have been found in small jugs in tombs from ancient Egypt.

This drug use had religious connections in antiquity. Some drug use has religious connections today. The most famous is peyote (pay-oh-TEE), the drug of some Native American religious observances in the American West. The right to use peyote has been challenged all the way to the United States Supreme Court. Legal injunctions against even its religious use are not likely to stop those for whom peyote is a part of their shamanistic religious observances.

Peyote, LSD, and other hallucinogenic drugs are used for religious purposes precisely because they do alter brain chemistry. These altered states are believed to induce a heightened religious consciousness. It is only in such a state that the user is enabled to receive the enlightenment he or she seeks. Drugs are believed by some to lead to deeper religious knowledge and understanding.

Satan Worship

In some circles whose members wish to be religious but at the same time have no use for God, worship of Satan has arisen. Satanists are fascinated with ritual and mystery, but many have come to an active hatred of God and Christianity. For this reason, many of the liturgies and rituals of Satan worship are intentional reversals, mirror images, of historical

Christian liturgies and rituals, as though those dedicated to Satan worship imagine they could negate God's power and destroy God's people by a reversal of Christian usages. Black masses include the sacrifice of goats on altars, ritual sexual acts on altars, desecration of crucifixes and other Christian objects, a "communion" that is a deliberate perversion of the Christian observance of the Last Supper, and other rituals twisted from Christian practices.

For the purposes of this survey, we must remember that Satan is a created being also. He was created as an exalted being, an archangel. So it would seem from the relatively few scriptural references to him. He may have been the highest of all created beings in the heavens, second only to God himself. However, Satan coveted the highest position for himself, so he rebelled against God and was cast out of heaven, along with numerous underlings he had persuaded to join him in rebellion.

Whatever this standard account of Satan's origins may mean in its details—and we have, after all, precious little detail in all the accounts put together—Satan is a powerful adversarial force in the world today. The name Satan means "adversary"; originally it was a Hebrew common noun, "adversary." Satan's worshipers are among the most outspoken adversaries of Christ and the Church today.

Yet at bottom, Satan worship is another manifestation of the human tendency to worship creation and the creature, rather than the Creator. This fallen creature Satan is, after all, only another being who ultimately is powerless before the creating, sustaining God who made him good before he rebelled. To worship Satan is only to worship something in nature.

Superstitions

Much of what we have looked at already has been called "superstitious" by many. Nevertheless, here we are noting a class of "small" or "unimportant" beliefs and actions concerned with avoiding "bad luck" and taking advantage of opportunities for "good luck" when they present themselves.

"Bad luck" events commonly known in North America include having a black cat walk across one's path, walking under a ladder, stepping on a crack in the sidewalk, spilling salt, breaking a mirror, the whole day of Friday the 13th, and almost anything that has the number 13 associated with it. Many hotels do not give the number 13 to the 13th floor. An old Russian belief is that to give a friend a knife will cut the friendship between the giver and the receiver, so the receiver of the knife gives the giver a penny.

"Good luck" events observed in North America include finding a four-leafed clover, carrying a rabbit's foot, finding a penny, and throwing salt over one's left shoulder if one has spilled salt. In Middle Eastern villages, doors and shutters often were painted blue in the past—one still can find them—to ward off the "evil eye" from the house.

Superstitious Blessings

Saying "God bless you" or "Gesundheit" when a person sneezes sounds harmless enough, and it may be. Many of us say it without a second thought. The origin of this custom lies in pagan European antiquity, however. It was thought that when one sneezes, the soul leaves the body. If the soul is to return, someone hearing the sneeze must say, "God bless you." Otherwise, it was thought, the sneezer would die. Whether a modern user of the phrase subscribes to that belief, or even knows about it, would vary from person to person, of course. Many people saying "Gesundheit" when you sneeze are only being polite.

Some people, as a matter of habit, say "good luck" when parting from someone or when one is beginning some enterprise or project. This can be traced at least as far back as Roman times, when Romans invoked the god Fortunatus to aid their enterprises. The average person today, when saying "good luck," probably is not aware of that connection. The question to be asked today is whether the speaker really believes in luck or merely is using a conventional phrase of well-wishing.

The Gods of Modern Society

Some of you reading this chapter may feel far removed from the neopaganism practices and beliefs we have outlined. While this perspective is mostly wishful thinking, it may be true that your life and your particular community may not commonly see the direct effects of pagan worship. However, there is another, more subtle and much more widespread form of paganism that is evident in every community. Paul Tillich, a modern theologian and philosopher, once described what God is with the phrase "Ultimate Concern." That which is of "ultimate concern" to us is our god. For Christians this is God himself. But for so many today, anything but God is their god—money, occupation, sports, possessions, and so forth. These gods are every bit as much a part of the pagan system of belief as the more obvious forms mentioned earlier—perhaps even more dangerous because they are so "acceptable." But the result of this kind of "worship" leads as surely to ultimate death as any other practice of worship that does not put God in first place.

Conclusion

This is but the briefest survey of beliefs and practices that occur in various forms around the world. Their common denominator is the belief that all nature is (or will be) god. Thus, all nature has spiritual powers that can act for good or ill toward human beings. This galaxy of beliefs can be grouped under the name "pantheism," which means "everything is god."

The belief is that those humans who find the secrets of currying favor with, or controlling, the gods and spirits lead more protected and successful lives, and often exercise control or influence over their less knowledgeable fellows. The various pantheistic systems promise personal success and power over others. These are coupled with promises of immortality, usually to be experienced as continual, unending reincarnations in this or a better world. To one who finds voluntary submission to God in Christ to be distasteful, exclusive, or too confining, these are alluring promises.

*Astrology, a false belief system, should not be confused with astronomy, a legitimate, scientific study of stars and planets.

Background Scripture: Proverbs 3:19-20; Ezekiel 13:17-23; Acts 19:23-28

About the Author: Dr. Joseph Coleson is professor of Old Testament at Nazarene Theological Seminary, Kansas City.

The United States Army has adopted as its marketing slogan the catchy phrase "Be all that you can be." This message reminds us that we all possess great potential to be successful people, if we will only allow our natural talents and abilities to grow and develop. Not many of us would dispute this encouraging statement. Some have taken this push to "be all that you can be" to the next level and have used the term "self-actualization" to describe the process of allowing everything we were created to be to become "actualized." The problem comes in when our desire to realize our full potential becomes the ultimate goal in our lives. When this happens we put our own selves as our priority, making ourselves "gods." This is a summary of the age-old philosophy we call New Age.

CHAPTER 8

The Challenge of the New Age Counterfeit

by Douglas R. Groothuis

TWENTY CHRISTIANS KNELT IN PRAYER the night before New Year's Eve. They came from different churches scattered throughout the greater Seattle area to meet at the office of a campus ministry. Many of them had not met before and probably would not meet again; yet they were one in purpose. They would get little sleep that night. It would be spiritual warfare; something had to be done.

Their aim was to confront the New Age movement with the gospel. Their target was the Seattle Kingdome, which from midnight until five in the morning would house the World Peace Event, sponsored by a host of New Age groups in the Seattle area. Similar events were being held worldwide with the hope of bringing peace through collective meditation. The idea was that if enough people would simultaneously harmonize their positive energy—at 12 noon, Greenwich mean time—this would create a "critical mass" of consciousness that would in turn paranormally galvanize and tranquilize the consciousness of the entire planet and catapult us into a New Age.

The hour began in the Kingdome with 20 minutes of highly repetitive "New Age music" followed by 10 minutes of silence; more music followed until, near 5 A.M., a chorus led the 7,000 pilgrims in a droning song, written for the event, called "We Are One Love." At the end of the song, the faithful throng lifted their hands over their heads . . . and it was over.

What Is Going On?

Just what is the New Age movement? And how has it affected our culture?

The New Age movement is not new; it is the most recent repeat of the second oldest religion, the spirituality of the serpent. Its rudiments were seductively sold to our first parents in the garden. Human pride was tickled, and it jumped.

The offer was to forsake God's way of life and to believe the serpent's promise that by rebelling against God, Adam and Eve could "be as gods" (Genesis 3:5, KJV) and would not die. In essence, they could gain power and knowledge apart from God and suffer no ill effect. Satan lied; Adam and Eve complied; and we all died.

"The New Age movement" is an umbrella term referring to a variety of people, organizations, events, practices, and ideas. Sociologically speaking, it is not a centrally organized movement with one human leader. Although it includes cults, sects, and even denominations, it is not restricted to any one of these. Rather, it is a constellation of like-minded people and groups all desiring a spiritual and social change that will usher in a New Age of self-actualization. Usually this scenario entails that we throw off both traditional monotheism (Judaism, Christianity, Islam) and secular humanism (rationalism, atheism, skepticism).[1]

The ideas and practices of the New Age also cover a broad range of plausibility. Some New Agers claim their ideas are supported by august disciplines such as quantum physics, while others embrace exotic beliefs with little concern for intellectual respectability.

Although the history of serpentine religion is as old as it is varied, its resurgence can be traced most recently in the West to the counterculture of the 1960s in America and Europe.[2]

At that time, ideas and practices traditionally held at bay by a Christian consensus (or the memory of one) began to burst on the scene. Youth overthrew as much of Western civilization as possible (stereos excepted). The West welcomed the East and tasted its mysteries. Mind-altering drugs were hailed as liberating. Sexual morality was first up for grabs and then down for the count. Besides introducing a score of new religious movements, the counterculture also fanned the embers of various Eastern, mystical, and occult ideas that had made their way westward since the 18th century.

The hippies may be gone, but the effect of the counterculture remains. The age of exotic, Eastern "guruism" may be waning, but the gurus' teachings are not. What was once on the little-known edge has moved into the spotlight.

The New Age is more than a passing fad—although it is not without faddishness. It is a deep cultural trend attracting scores of people from all walks of life. It claims to offer spiritual reality, fulfillment, and world harmony. Yet its promises spring from what turns out to be a spiritual counterfeit.

To sort the genuine from the counterfeit requires biblical discernment, not just the identification of New Age buzzwords. A rich knowledge of the genuine article—biblical Christianity—throws the counterfeit into clear relief.

Despite the diversity within the New Age movement, several of its unifying ideas can be distilled into its basic worldview, which are summarized below into nine beliefs or doctrines.

Evolutionary Optimism: A Counterfeit Kingdom

The New Age movement teaches that we are poised on the edge of a quantum leap in consciousness as evolution surges upward. We face a great time of both planetary crisis and opportunity. Some New Agers sound apocalyptic tones, warning that without a massive raising of consciousness, the planet will face severe catastrophes that will "cleanse" it from error. Some individuals and groups expect a world leader, sometimes (falsely) called "the Christ," to show us the way to the New Age. Others emphasize personal direction and shun any outside guidance.

Christians have traditionally confessed the Creator God as Lord over history. We turn to Him and His Word for social righteousness, as well as for personal salvation and holiness. Christians live in the anticipation that history will culminate in a literal, physical, and visible return of Jesus Christ in power and glory and not in a New Age brought about by some immanent evolutionary process.

Monism: A Counterfeit Cosmos

All is one. One is all. The musical refrain for the World Peace Event mentioned earlier was "we are one love; we are one." The event was geared toward this "realization"—there is no separation, there are no ultimate boundaries, we are but waves in one cosmic ocean.

The idea that all is one—monism—is contrary to the biblical view of God's creation as a wondrous diversity of created things. Genesis 1:2 records that at the onset of God's creation "the earth was formless and empty." He spoke the word, and plurality burst forth in trees, animals, clouds, humans, and a million things more. "God saw all [plural] that he had made, and it was very good" (v. 31). The New Age viewpoint, in a sense, seeks to return to the formless and empty primeval soup and sink into it.

All things have a common Creator and are sustained by Christ (Hebrews 1:3). In this sense we live in a *uni*verse, not a *multi*verse. God unifies history according to His will, but the unity of God's plan does not destroy the real differences in His creation. Likewise, Jesus taught the unity of His followers as the Body of Christ (John 17), as did Paul (1 Corinthians 12:12-31), and yet this unity is not the undifferentiated oneness taught by the New Age. All people will one day stand before their Maker as individuals. None will have their case dismissed by dissolving into the great "ocean of being."

Pantheism: A Counterfeit God and Humanity

Pantheism believes all that exists is god. That is an impersonal view of God, "not the personal Judeo-Christian God, but some more abstract entity, usually capitalized, like 'Infinite Intelligence,' 'Principle,' etc."[3] We could add to this list "the Force," "Consciousness," "Energy," and so on. The New Age god is not a moral being worshiped as supreme. Such a god is an impersonal and amoral *it,* not a personal being. Furthermore, deity is democratized—we are all god.

Transformation of Consciousness: Counterfeit Conversion

It is not enough merely to believe New Age teachings. They must be experienced. New Agers are often encouraged to be *initiated,* not just *interested.* Many mystical means serve the same exotic end, whether they be non-Christian meditation techniques, drugs, yoga, martial arts, the use of crystals, or spontaneous experiences such as near-death encounters. The end is a feeling of oneness with everything that is and the realization of one's own divinity, sometimes called the "Higher Self."

Rather than preaching repentance from sin, the New Age pushes reawakening to self. The New Age counterfeit replaces prayer (communication with a personal God) with Eastern meditation (the journey within the self). It exalts experience of self above faith in Christ and thus is a counterfeit of genuine Christian conversion. Instead of teaching the necessity of being born again from above, it teaches the rediscovery of the true, inner, and divine self that already resides in each of us.

Create Your Own Reality: Counterfeit Morality

The phrase "create your own reality" is often intoned in New Age circles as a basic premise. The idea is that we are not under any objective moral law. Rather, we all have different ways to realize our divine potential. And since "all is one" (monism), we can't slice up life into categories such as good versus evil. That is too dualistic; we must move beyond good and evil in order to realize our full potential. If New Agers assert moral absolutes, they usually do so more instinctively than reflectively. Some may speak of the law of karma as regulating moral rewards and punishments in reincarnation, but the notion of morality is usually relativized or jettisoned entirely.

Biblical morality is anchored in the unchanging moral character and will of a personal God, who has issued the Ten Commandments, not the 10 suggestions. Christians become more spiritual in thought, character, and deed by obeying the will of their Lord, not by pretending to create their own rules as they go along.

Unlimited Human Potential: Counterfeit Miracles

If we are all god, then the prerogatives of deity pulsate within. We are endowed beyond measure. We are miracles waiting to happen. Untethered from such old-age "fables" as human finitude, depravity, and original sin, we are free to explore the luminous horizons of godhood. Ignorance is our only problem. Knowledge of "the god within" results in power over all.

The Bible warns of the reality of counterfeit miracles malevolently engineered by Satan. A supernatural Creator can and does miraculously intervene in His creation for the purpose of demonstrating His reality; yet counterfeits abound, deceiving the world.

Spirit Contact: Counterfeit Revelations

There is a galaxy of masters, entities, spirits, extraterrestrials, and other talkative types who communicate through automatic writing or vocalization through mediums—who are more recently called "channelers" (an apt title for the television age). Channeling has always been tied up with the New Age but is now gaining more popularity as channelers address large audiences and engage in extensive private consultations.

New Age channeling adds a "higher" dimension to the older spiritualism movement of a century ago, which was often content to summon the departed spirit of a relative for a few postmortem comments concerning accommodations in the afterlife. According to one New Age writer, "this new kind of channeling" concerns messages that seem to come from "a higher source . . . that deals with universal principles or laws."[4] Thus, channeling becomes a counterfeit of biblical prophecy because the true prophets in the Bible were sent by God to proclaim His universal truth, not just particular bits of information.[5]

Such "revelations" cause us to remember the apostle Paul's stern warning that "even if we or an angel from heaven should preach a gospel other than the one we preached to you, let him be eternally condemned!" (Galatians 1:8). The channeled "gospel" is one of self-deification, relativism, and reincarnation.

Masters from Above: Counterfeit Angels

In much of New Age thought, the distinction between the extraterrestrial and the spiritual is blurred when UFO sightings and even encounters "of the third kind" become mystical experiences. UFOs (and their passengers) are sometimes claimed to exhibit paranormal phenomena.

Those supposedly contacted by the UFOs often display traits common in other kinds of occult phenomena such as a trance state, automatic writing, peering into crystals, the poltergeist (noisy ghost) effect, levitation, psychic control, psychic healing, and out-of-body experiences.[6]

Syncretism: Counterfeit Religion

New Age spirituality is a rather eclectic grab bag of Eastern mysticism, Western occultism, neopaganism, and human potential psychology. Yet New Age spokespeople tend to view the true essence of all religion to be one. An appeal is made to a supposedly mystical core that unites all religions: All is one; all is god; we are god; we have infinite potential; we can bring in the New Age.

Christians reject syncretism (this combining of unrelated factors) on at least three counts. First, it disregards the historical differences between religions. Second, it distorts Christianity by making it fit onto a pantheistic Procrustean bed.[7] Third, it demotes Jesus Christ to merely one of many masters, a position He expressly denied by claiming to be "the way and the truth and the life" (John 14:6).[8]

Rather than being a mere fad, the New Age movement is a substantial cultural trend that is not destined quickly to blow away in the wind. It offers Christians a deep challenge to unmask and lovingly confront a very potent spiritual counterfeit.

---

1. Douglas Groothuis, *Unmasking the New Age* (Downers Grove, Ill.: InterVarsity Press, 1986), 93-109.

2. The best Christian critique of the counterculture is by Os Guinness in *The Dust of Death* (Downers Grove, Ill.: InterVarsity Press, 1975).

3. Robert S. Ellwood, *Religious and Spiritual Groups in Modern America* (Englewood Cliffs, N.J.: Prentice-Hall, 1973), 29.

4. Brad Steiger, *Revelation: The Divine Fire* (Englewood Cliffs, N.J.: Prentice-Hall, 1973), 42-43.

5. Abraham Heschel, *The Prophets* (U.S.A.: Jewish Publication Society of America, 1962), 472.

6. Jacques Valle, *Messengers of Deception* (New York: Bantam, 1980), 33, 224-25.

7. A scheme or pattern into which someone or something is arbitrarily forced.

8. Groothuis, *Unmasking the New Age,* 146-57.

Background Scripture: Genesis 1:2, 31; 3:5; John 14:6; 17:1-26; 1 Corinthians 12:12-31; Galatians 1:8; Hebrews 1:3

This chapter adapted and reprinted from *Confronting the New Age* by Douglas Groothuis. © 1988 by Douglas Groothuis. Used by permission of InterVarsity Press, P.O. Box 1400, Downers Grove, IL 60515.

In the Book of Hebrews, at the very beginning of the well-loved "faith" chapter, chapter 11, we read a definition of faith: "Now faith is being sure of what we hope for and certain of what we do not see" (v. 1). We talk much about faith when we talk about our spiritual journey. The word "faith" is perhaps the most used theological word in all of the New Testament. We know that without faith no one will see God; but how do we get a handle on something "we do not see"? Faith is one of those aspects of our spiritual life that we dare not take for granted simply for lack of definition, for by it we are offered a window on the supernatural. In this chapter we will establish some useful foundation points to help us understand better what we mean by Christian faith. As He called Peter, our Lord will call us to "walk on the waves," to increase our faith in the One who offers His unseen hand to those who believe.

CHAPTER 9

Christian Faith

by Mark A. Holmes

IN MY PARENTS' HOME there is a food storage area in the back corner of the basement. Among the many goodies there is an old refrigerator in which they keep a supply of soft drinks. On different occasions, when I have been home to visit, I have gone down to this refrigerator to get a can of refreshment. Though I would not consider the trip an actual pilgrimage, in one sense it is an expression of faith. I set out believing that my parents' claims are true—I will find a soft drink at this particular place in their home. They could be lying. There may not be a soda, refrigerator, storage, or even a basement under the house. It is because of their statement that I set out. To verify its truthfulness, I need only use my five senses, open the basement door, descend the steps, walk to the back corner, and open the refrigerator. So far I have always found the promised refreshment, though I would admit to being disappointed in the selection of soft drinks from time to time.

All right, I agree that getting a soft drink from a refrigerator in a basement is not a great leap of faith. Yet, it does reveal that, even in the most simple of day-to-day activities, a measure of faith is exercised.

Faith is that means by which we embrace the reality of something that exists beyond our ability to verify by natural means. In the Christian context, faith is the means by which we relate to God. The writer of the Book of Hebrews defines Christian faith as "being sure of what we hope for and certain of what we do not see" (11:1). Faith in this expression is the means by which we embrace the reality of the world that exists beyond our natural realm, a world whose boundaries extend beyond our sensual perception and even our rational verification. We refer to this realm as the supernatural because it extends beyond nature itself. Christians believe that God dwells within the supernatural, existing as He always has and always will, beyond our natural senses. Though we may not see, touch, taste, hear, or smell Him, faith enables us to embrace His existence as fact.

This faith is not the result of speculation but of revelation. Revelation is the supernatural disclosed to us in ways we can understand, and comes to us in several forms. *Natural revelation* is the experience we can have observing an aspect of creation, resulting in a sense that a greater truth exists beyond the immediate experience. Often this is expressed as we watch a sunset, view a mountain scene, or gaze into the heavens at night, becoming aware that behind all that is seen exists a divine being.

Another form of revelation is called *special revelation.* This tends to be more hazy, resulting from impressions, dreams, mental awareness, visions, voices, and so forth. Special revelation is the result of God breaking into our physical world with an action or message of truth.

A third major source of revelation is the *Bible.* Christians believe that the Bible is a supernaturally inspired Book that God led human authors to write. Christians believe God reveals His nature and His will to us within the Bible's words and accounts.

Yet, though God reveals himself to us in these various ways, it still requires faith on our part as believers to embrace their claims as true. Faith is the major component in the Christian life, for by it we both understand and experience God, His will for us, and His benevolent interaction within our world and our personal lives. God has made a number of revelations that have become a basis for much of what we believe about Him. These expressions are distinctives of the

Christian faith that establish the uniqueness of our belief over and against the claims of other religions. Understanding the distinctions of these revelations gives us clarity in what we believe and why. To help in understanding the distinctives of the Christian faith, let us consider several of the major revelations God has made.

God as Creator and Person

Of primary importance in the Christian faith is the belief that there exists within the supernatural realm a divine personality we call God. While God is indeed supreme and exercises a powerful influence over His creation, He continually shares His existence as person. He is not an inanimate power or an impersonal force, but a personal reality. To help us understand this, God refers to himself in Scripture by personal expressions: He is our *Father* (Deuteronomy 32:6; Psalm 2:7; Isaiah 63:16; Jeremiah 3:19) and *Shepherd* (Genesis 48:15; Psalm 23:1; Isaiah 40:11).

His most prevalent references in Scriptures are by masculine pronouns, presenting His identity as male, though some have shown clearly that God comprises the best of male and female qualities; many of the biblical images for God show distinct "mothering" aspects to His care (e.g., a mother hen gathering her young). We are also told in Genesis 1:26 that we were made in God's image. While this does not mean God looks like a human, the personal attributes of God are reflected in our own ability to reason, love, appreciate beauty, plan, show compassion, and so forth. These are traits we associate as personal that find their origin in God.

Christians have come to understand that this personhood of God has three expressions—referred to as the Trinity—namely the Father, Son, and Holy Spirit. Each of these is God, yet a unique expression that reveals God to humankind, allowing us to relate to Him in faith.

Jesus Christ the Son

Jesus Christ is the "Son" of the Trinity of God. The Christian faith has always believed that He is completely God, yet He became completely human and lived among us. This has caused a problem for some movements because it goes beyond reason. In an attempt to explain this, various views have been developed that usually play down the divinity aspect (making Jesus a good teacher, prophet, or lesser god) or play down the humanity side (recognizing His divinity while claiming He was not really a man, only appearing to be a man). If Jesus was not God and only a good man, He could not be an effectual sacrifice for the sins of humankind. No matter how good He could be, no mere human is guiltless of sin (Romans 3:9-18, 23). Therefore He could not be a pure sacrifice for the sin of humankind. His death would simply have been what He deserved, like the rest of us.

The Christian faith believes that Jesus Christ, being fully God and fully human at the same time, came to earth for two main purposes: (1) to reveal to us the nature of God through His life (John 14:9; 10:30, 38); and (2) to fulfill the salvation plan of God, determined from before Creation, by His willful, sacrificial death for the sins of humankind (Ephesians 1:3-14). This sacrifice for sins is a faith issue. As we claim His death by faith to be our own, our sins are forgiven.

The fact that Jesus died for our sins does not mean He no longer exists. Christians believe that the Father raised Jesus from the dead, restoring in Him not only His life but also the full glory that He had before time through His ascension back to heaven (Ephesians 1:19-23).

The Holy Spirit

As the third person of the Trinity, the Holy Spirit is understood to be active within our present world. Although referred to as Spirit, one must be careful not to rob from Him His identity as person. The Holy Spirit is not an "It" but a

"He." The Holy Spirit is not just a force or influence but a personal entity that relates to humankind.

A careful distinction needs to be made regarding the holy influence of God within humanity. As it was popular once, it has become fashionable again, especially in the New Age movement, to become aware of God's presence and influence in this world and our lives. However, this awareness is errantly explained as recognizing a godlike entity within us that is natural or innate. We are called to become aware of the divine within, but the Holy Spirit is not an innate part of humankind. He is a personality all His own, who enters and indwells believers.

The presence of the Holy Spirit is a faith exercise requiring one to accept Jesus' promise to His disciples as true. However, it is not without its validations. The presence of the Holy Spirit can be confirmed several ways. There is a personal witness to the believer by the Spirit himself, "The Spirit himself testifies with our spirit that we are God's children" (Romans 8:16). There are the fruits of the Spirit, which Paul refers to in Galatians 5:22-23, that influence the personality of the believer by love, joy, peace, patience, kindness, longsuffering, and so forth. The presence of the Holy Spirit can be evidenced by certain abilities, referred to as "gifts," given to equip the believer for ministry (Ephesians 4:11-13).

The Church

It is easy for us to mistakenly limit our understanding of church to mean a particular building, group of people, or even a denomination or movement. In the broadest sense, the Church is the title given to God's children worldwide. The original Greek word used for Church in the Scriptures is *ecclesia*, which literally means the "called-out ones." Being called out is the experience of the Christian as the Holy Spirit has revealed to us God's provision for salvation and fellowship. To embrace this salvation, we are required to respond faithfully by stepping out of the sinful life we are presently living, renouncing the errant ways of the world, and living by the directives of God's kingdom. The Church is the provision of God where we are to gather, find identity, worship, and live in mutual encouragement with one another (Hebrews 10:24-25).

Forgiveness of Sins

There is probably no greater area where the exercise of faith comes to play for the Christian than in the forgiveness of sins. Sin, as understood by the Christian faith, is the transgression of God's will—doing a "thou shalt not" or failing to do a "thou shalt." We understand that God is perfect and in Him there is no sin, nor can God entertain sin without expressing judgment against it. Since, as the Scriptures point out, all of humankind has sinned before God (Romans 3:23), we all find ourselves recipients of God's judgment. This would remain unchangeably true were it not for God's great love providing a means by which we can escape this judgment by seeking forgiveness for our sins. This forgiveness is made possible by the death of Jesus Christ as explained earlier in this chapter. If we accept this claim by faith, God forgives us instead of judging us.

Ephesians 2:5 and 8 reveal two effective words for the Christian's understanding of salvation—*grace* and *faith*. Grace we know to be unmerited favor. God, by all rights, would be just in dealing severely with us for our sins against Him. Yet because of His love and Jesus' sacrifice, He chooses to extend unmerited favor and proclaim that we are forgiven, making us His children. We do not deserve this kind treatment. That is why we recognize it as an act of grace. We have nothing that can be contributed toward our salvation outside of our willingness to accept and credit this graceful act to God.

Bodily Resurrection

A Christian distinction regarding the disposition of the individual after death deals with the state by which the believer is resurrected. This topic is often a place of confusion brought on by the influence of early Greek ideas introduced into our beliefs. The Greeks held the view that there was a strong division that needed to be maintained between the physical and nonphysical world. Flesh and spirit were not only two different entities of existence, they were also opposites in conflict with each other. To the Greeks, flesh was evil and spirit was good. The task of a human was to so live as to be freed eventually from the evil encasement of flesh so that he or she could become a free spirit unencumbered by sinful flesh. Eventually, those who achieved this purity of spirit would, upon death, be released from the flesh, allowing their spirits to return to heaven.

A modern, Christianized view of this Greek influence interprets the soul's release from the flesh at death and its return to God. However, God reveals through Scripture that the resurrection experience is not the release of spirit from flesh but the embodiment of the soul in a new, unique body. Our primary example of this is seen in Jesus Christ in His resurrected state. From what was written, it is obvious that Jesus was more than a phantom spirit appearing to His followers. He had form and substance. It is implied that Mary Magdalene could have embraced Jesus at the tomb (John 20:17). He walked and talked with the confused disciples to Emmaus, eventually revealing His identity by breaking bread during their meal together (Luke 24:13-35). He encouraged Thomas in his doubt to touch His wounded hands and thrust his hand into His spear-ripped side (John 20:26-27). He made a fire and breakfast by the Sea of Galilee for His disciples (21:9-10). All of these suggest that the resurrected state of Jesus was more than spirit; He had a body as well. By earthly standards, it was an unusual body, for it could disappear into and appear from nothing (20:19).

Eternal Life

Just about every religion has a belief that includes eternal existence for humankind. To some, eternal life is a process where one returns to this world to live again, either as another human or some other created being. Known as "reincarnation," this belief would understand eternal life as the ongoing experience of this present world in different forms at different times. Christianity does not believe in reincarnation because the Scriptures are quite clear that the life lived after this present experience is contained within the supernatural realm. Humankind is to die but once, after which we come before God for our eternal disposition (Hebrews 9:27).

To the Christian, human life is eternal. Once conceived, one's life may experience different states of existence, being moved by various processes from one to another, but life is an ongoing, eternal reality. From conception, life begins experiencing the mystery of gestation, which is a process that changes us from a single cell to the multimillion cell form we are accustomed to seeing every day. At birth, our existence is transferred from the environment of the womb into the new experience of life in this world. At death, as explained above, we go through a transition where our living entities move from this present body, which has failed us, to a spiritual body supplied to us by God. In this state, we will experience eternity, life without end.

It is not a question for Christians *whether* we will live forever, but *where* we will live. As explained in Scripture, at life's end here on earth, we are raised in a spiritual body to come before God as He will pronounce upon us our deserved fate. Those who have accepted His salvation through Jesus Christ will be welcomed into the Kingdom prepared for eternal fellowship with God. However, those who spurned this grace of salvation will be given the ultimate end of their desires, life away from the influence and benefit of God. Hell is their banishment, and there they will dwell in torment for eternity.

Prayer

Prayer is that blessed experience Christians exercise that allows us to communicate with God directly. It is so common an activity that its awesome privilege often escapes us, even sometimes is treated as trivial. If we really allowed the thought of our experience in prayer to sink into our consciousness, perhaps our activity in this area would change. Prayer is the activity that allows us to enter into the very throne room of God and speak to the King of Kings and Lord of Lords as we would to our fathers.

I have never been inside the White House in Washington, D.C. Maybe someday I will take the tour made available to people, but I doubt I will ever be ushered in before the president who lives and works there. Even if I wanted to talk with him, it is doubtful that I would be given any of his valuable time. I would no doubt be referred to an assistant. In prayer, we are not talking about the president of the United States, we are communicating with the Creator of the universe, the One who spoke and all things came into existence, and the One who could just as easily speak and all things would cease to exist. To this One, we are allowed free access.

The beauty of prayer is we are allowed before God the Father because His Son, Jesus Christ, is continually in the Father's presence, praying in intercession for us. In evidence before the Father are the wounds of love our Savior bears. Charles Wesley captured this scene in his hymn "Arise, My Soul, Arise."

> *Five bleeding wounds He bears,*
> *Received on Calvary.*
> *They pour effectual prayers;*
> *They strongly plead for me.*
> *"Forgive him, O forgive," they cry.*
> *"Forgive him, O forgive," they cry,*
> *"Nor let that ransomed sinner die."*

Christians have the boldness to enter the throne room of God the Father because we do so through the merits and sacrifice of Jesus Christ, His Son and our Intercessor. That is why it is most appropriate to include in our prayers the statement that we come to God through Jesus Christ the Son. We have the ability to enter and be heard, without fear of judgment, as we come with the blood of Christ upon us. To such, God always extends His welcome.

In keeping with the full expression of the Trinity, we have seen how the Father is the recipient of our prayers and how Jesus is the avenue through which we are allowed access to God. The Holy Spirit is the means by which we pray. There is something altogether lovely about this provision. God is so aware of our limitations and inabilities that He has provided every aspect of our fellowship with Him, even our prayer life. It is by or in the Spirit that we effectively pray. As the Spirit makes known to us the heart and mind of God, He also makes known to God the heart and mind of the individual (Romans 8:27)—even in those situations where we have no words to share because of grief that is too great. We are promised that the Holy Spirit intercedes for us by groans (v. 26).

I believe I witnessed this once in my early ministry. A man lost his wife and three daughters in a tragic car crash. Only he and a son were left from this family of six people. I assisted in the funeral and walked behind this grief-stricken man as he was led away from the church to the waiting car that would take him to the cemetery. As I walked, I could hear from deep within this man a groaning with each step he took. Immediately I felt a sense that these were not mere mortal sounds, and the words of Paul came to my mind. Oh, the privileges of prayer to those who believe! We have an Almighty God, who extends to us an open audience; a Divine Sacrifice, who intercedes with His blood; and an ever-present Comforter, who makes possible our most feeble attempts to converse with God.

So many things could be discussed regarding the Christian benefit and experience of faith. Literally, there is no aspect of our relationship with God that is not influenced and controlled by it. It is the means of believing and accepting what is not verifiable in this world, a window into the supernatural. It is also the avenue by which we benefit the full provision and experience of God in our life. As we embrace these unique distinctions of God's revelation to us, through faith, so our lives are changed and enriched by the One to whom our faith is extended.

Background Scripture: Genesis 1:26; 48:15; Deuteronomy 32:6; Psalms 2:7; 23:1; Isaiah 40:11; 63:16; Jeremiah 3:19; Luke 24:13-35; John 10:30, 38; 14:9; 20:17, 19, 26-27; 21:9-10; Romans 3:9-18, 23; 8:16, 26-27; Ephesians 1:3-14, 19-23; 2:5, 8; 4:11-13; Hebrews 9:27; 10:24-25; 11:1

About the Author: Rev. Mark A. Holmes is senior pastor of Darrow Road Wesleyan Church in Superior, Wisconsin.

Grandma's house was fun to visit. So many unique sights and smells; each left its indelible imprint on my young mind. One sight was particularly powerful. It was a small, black plaque with bold white words that quoted the well-known Christian motto: "Prayer Changes Things." I have often relied on the truth of this assertion in times when prayer was the only way things that needed to be changed could be changed. Over the years, I have thought about that phrase many times, and it still is true—prayer *does* change things. Yet, as I have matured in my walk with Christ, I think I have discovered a prayer motto that is perhaps even more important and maybe more true than the motto I read on Grandma's wall: Prayer Changes Me. At the heart of prayer is a desire to bridge the spiritual gap between the divine and the human and to bring God's will into complete harmony with our hearts and minds.

CHAPTER 10

Christian Prayer

by George Lyons

SIMPLY PUT, prayer is a human's communication with God. Our concern is to understand the proper way to pray as Christians and what we should expect from prayer. How should we pray, and what does prayer do?

In one sense, prayer is inevitable. Whether one likes it or not, believes it or not, God exists. And everyone, aware of it or not, lives and moves and exists in the inescapable presence of God. Every word we speak, every thought we think, every aspiration we cherish are fully known to God. There are times when we are more or less aware of God's presence, but there is nowhere God is not present (see Psalm 139:7-12). Whether we admit it or not, we humans live in total dependence upon God. He alone is the Creator. All else that exists is His creation and is sustained by His power and providence. Explicitly or implicitly, well or poorly, everyone prays.

Some say in deed or word, "God, I don't care what You want. I don't need You. I don't want You around. Leave me alone." And God hears such misguided prayers. Although He does not force himself into the consciousness of such people, He does not abandon them, despite their rude rejection of Him. For if He did, they would cease to exist.

Others say in deed or word, "God, give me what I want, but let me live as I please." God may even answer such selfish prayers. Yet our hearts' deepest desires, apart from God, are never really satisfying.

Still others say in deed and word, "God, I need You more than life itself. Apart from You, my world will fall apart. Save me." And God hears such desperate prayers.

Everyone prays. The question is not *whether* but *how well* we pray. Praying well is not a matter of the precision, posture, or place of prayer. Praying well requires us to keep in mind the Person to whom we pray and the purpose of prayer.

Precision, Posture, and Place of Prayer

Praying well does not require that we keep a thesaurus in hand, choosing our words cautiously to get the precise nuance we intend to communicate. It is not a matter of the vocabulary or grammar of prayer. We do not need to take lessons in speaking Elizabethan English so as to get our "Thees" and "Thous," our "doests" and "doths" just right. God knows our hearts. The Holy Spirit can take even the inarticulate groaning of one who does not know what to pray and interpret such prayers flawlessly to the Father (see Romans 8:26-27).

Every culture has its own sense of the proper body language of prayer. The Bible was thousands of years in the making, and the people of the Bible were influenced by a variety of cultures. So we should not be surprised that the Bible refers to a number of different postures of prayer. Whether we pray with uplifted hands and eyes; folded hands, bowed head, and closed eyes; standing, kneeling, or prostrate on the ground, all these nonverbal expressions are a part of the communication act we call prayer. The various bodily expressions of prayer communicate our supplication before, dependence on, reverence for, humility before, or submission to God. As the examples of the Bible show, there is no "correct" posture for prayer.

The Bible likewise reports the prayers of God's people being expressed in a variety of places—indoors and outdoors, in barren deserts and on mountaintops, in caves and open fields, on dry land and at sea, in sanctuaries and in everyday places. There is apparently no place where prayer is out of place.

Proper Prayers

So what is the point about praying well? There are many ways to pray, and pious-sounding words are not what constitutes prayer. Still, there *are* wrong ways to pray, and we should avoid them. Jesus said that His disciples should not pray like the hypocrites. In secular Greek, the term *hypokritai* referred to actors. Hypocrites are people who pray more to impress others than to speak with God. Is their piety only a charade—a performance intended to deceive others?

The problem with the prayers of these hypocrites was apparently not that they failed to practice what they preached. It was not that they urged others to pray but failed to do so themselves. On the contrary, they loved to pray, but for all the wrong reasons. The problem with the prayers of these hypocrites was not that they prayed standing. Nor was it with the place where they prayed—"in the synagogues and on the street corners" (Matthew 6:5). The problem was that their prayers were long, pretentious, and forgetful of God (Luke 20:47).

Public prayer. Although Jesus preferred to pray alone (see, for example, Luke 3:21-22; 9:18, 28; 11:1; John 11:41-42), the Gospels report that He prayed at times in places where His prayers were publicly witnessed and overheard by others. His earliest followers prayed in public (see, for example, Matthew 18:19; Mark 11:17; Acts 1:24; 3:1; 14:23; 1 Corinthians 14:13-19). It was apparently in the presence of a group that Jesus first uttered the words we know as the Lord's Prayer (Matthew 6:9-10). So it should not be surprising that this model prayer presumes a corporate setting. We are taught to say not *"My* Father" but *"Our* Father."

Private prayer. Jesus urged His disciples to pray in "your room" (6:6). This could refer to a storeroom or "closet" (KJV), but more likely it refers simply to an "inner room" (NASB), undisturbed by the activity outside—a quiet, private setting for personal prayer. Jesus opposed the public setting of private prayers preferred by "pious" Jews of His day. Devotions are times for intimate communion with God, not opportunities to flaunt one's spirituality.

Jesus presumed that His disciples would enjoy an intimate—personal and private—relationship with the God "who is unseen" (v. 6). We can find God anywhere, even in secluded spots. And He knows everything we do, even in private.

Jesus promises that the Father will reward private prayers (v. 6). This might seem to guarantee that disciples will receive everything they ask for, at least if they are within the will of God (see Matthew 7:7-11; 1 John 3:21-22; 5:14-15). Yet in the present context, He must mean only that God, as opposed to human admirers, will recognize the genuineness of our spirituality. The reward of prayer is private communion with God, even if we never get exactly what we ask for.

Pretense. The problem with the prayers of hypocrites was their calculated efforts to arrange the time and place of their prayers to be seen by people. They sought an audience of admirers, not an audience with God. Their motives for praying were misguided. When they got the admiration they sought from the crowd, they received their reward in full. They were to expect nothing more from God. The hypocrisy Jesus condemned in Matthew 6 was not self-conscious deception at all. Perhaps the only ones these hypocrites deceived were themselves.

At a church gathering 30 years ago, I watched in disbelief as a table full of Christians knelt beside their chairs in a restaurant and prayed in full voice before eating their meals. I sincerely doubt they said grace at home in such an ostentatious manner. God is the judge, not I, as to whether their prayers were sincere or only intended to impress others with their "Christian witness." Sadly, I must admit that on more than one occasion I have bowed my head before a meal and said not one genuine word of thanks to God. Years of habitual prayers may become hypocritical prayers—a mere outward display of piety that fails to communicate with God.

Jesus expected something other of His disciples than

merely a parade of public piety (see Matthew 5:20). His concern was not with their *reputation* as religious persons but with the *reality* of their character. God's opinion of them was more crucial than the opinions of others.

Pagan prayers. Jesus also warned His disciples not to "pray . . . like pagans" (6:7). Disciples were not to pray expecting to earn the attention of God.

People who don't know God "keep on babbling" when they pray. The Greek word translated here is from *battalogeo.* It is a compound word. The second part refers to speaking. The first has no precise meaning. It is a word that sounds like what it means, like our words "meow" and "crackle." The barbarian tongue sounded like "batta, batta, batta" to Greek-speakers. In fact, the Greek word translated "barbarian" (*barbaros*) is another similar word, meaning one who says "bar-bar."

The problem with pagan prayers might be that they are only "empty phrases" (RSV) or "meaningless words" (TEV). If the point is to avoid mindless chatter or gibberish when praying, Jesus' warning may address the abuse of glossalalia, "speaking in tongues" (see 1 Corinthians 14:14-15). Later in the Sermon on the Mount, Jesus makes it clear that charismatic gifts are no guarantee of entrance to heaven (Matthew 7:21-23).

But *battalogeo* may refer to lengthy prayers or "vain repetitions" (KJV)—saying "the same prayer over and over" (TLB). At least Jesus explains their practice in this way: "They think they will be heard because of their many words" (6:7). And yet, Jesus insists elsewhere that people "should always pray and not give up" (Luke 18:1). How can unceasing, persistent prayer avoid being lengthy or repetitious?

Persistent prayer. The call for persistent prayer does not imply that God only reluctantly answers prayer. It is not to say, "Keep at it. You'll eventually wear God down, and He'll cave in and give you what you want." It simply encourages prayerfulness. If an inconvenienced and annoyed friend gives an impolite neighbor what he needs, how much more is God delighted to hear and answer our prayers (see Luke 11:5-10).

If a crooked judge will render a just verdict to a powerless woman who refuses to give up, how much more will God answer our prayers! (see Luke 18:1-8).

Those whose prayers seem to go unanswered should keep on praying, without resorting to nagging. God is far more gracious than any friend and far more just than any judge. He will answer our prayers. God's willingness to answer is the basis for confidence in prayer. Disciples may ask God for anything they need with the assurance that He is more eager to give than they are to request it.

Preoccupation with prayer. Perhaps the point of Jesus' claim that people should always pray is that prayer is to be more than an interruption in the routine of our lives. It is to be the hallmark of the lives of disciples. Prayer is not simply something religious we do when we're not doing anything else. It is something we are always doing.

The apostle Paul calls us to pray without ceasing. His own testimony shows this is not simply an impossible ideal. In half a dozen passages in Paul's letters, he claims that he never stops praying (Romans 1:9; Ephesians 1:16; Colossians 1:9; 1 Thessalonians 1:2-3; 2:13; 2 Timothy 1:3). We know that Paul did not spend all of his time in a private prayer closet, alone on his knees. He obviously spent time in other activities as well—making tents to make a living, preaching to make converts, and teaching to make disciples out of converts. Some of Paul's time must have been spent in eating, drinking, sleeping, traveling, writing letters, and other ordinary activities.

To be ever prayerful is the opposite of being prideful. It is to have learned to live in self-conscious dependence on God (see 2 Corinthians 1:9). It is to be free of the illusion of self-sufficiency. This is the attitude of gratitude and expectancy, which is the atmosphere of the life of prayer. Only in this sense can we make sense of Paul's injunction to "pray continually" (1 Thessalonians 5:17).

The attitude of gratitude and expectancy enables us, in

Paul's words, to "devote [ourselves] to prayer, being watchful and thankful" (Colossians 4:2). To pray without ceasing is to live on the basis of faith, hope, and love. It is to rejoice in God's daily deliverance of ourselves and others. It is to tap the resources of God's unfailing promises. Thus, we "pray in the Spirit on all occasions with all kinds of prayers and requests, . . . alert and always . . . praying" (Ephesians 6:18).

Prayer was not an interruption in Paul's normal activities; it was his normal activity. Paul knew a kind of prayer that was unceasing, fervent, and comprehensive of all of life. In this realization, he was simply following Jesus' advice and example, a life of total submission to and unswerving trust in God.

Petition. The distinguishing feature of Christian prayer is the certainty that God our Father knows what we need before we ask Him (Matthew 6:8). Thus, prayer is not to be confused with sending a Christmas list to the Cosmic Santa Claus. It is not like placing an order with the Heavenly Waiter. It is not telling God what to do. Jesus' followers are to "seek first [God's] kingdom and his righteousness." Then they can rest assured that all they really need—food, drink, and clothing—"will be given" to them (6:25-33).

Trust in God's wisdom and love does not make prayer unnecessary. It is, instead, the basis for confidence in prayer. Disciples may petition God for good things because they are persuaded that He is more eager to give these things than any human father (7:11). "Therefore," Jesus says, "I tell you, whatever you ask for in prayer, believe that you have received it, and it will be yours" (Mark 11:24).

And yet, believing prayer is not the magic that moves heaven to act. God is more willing and more able to give than His children are willing and able to ask (see Ephesians 3:20). Nevertheless, He is too wise and loving to give them everything they ask for (see 2 Corinthians 12:7-10). Sometimes, "you do not have, because you do not ask God." At other times, "when you ask, you do not receive, because you ask with wrong motives" (James 4:2-3).

Purpose of Prayer

If prayer is communication with God, its purpose is not so much to get things from God as it is to enter into the wholesome relationship with God that the Bible describes as peace. God desires our fellowship. Our primary motivation for prayer should be to get to know Him more intimately, to become so in-tune with Him that we work with Him to see His will accomplished in our own lives, in His Church, and in this fallen world. In prayer, we learn what God loves, what breaks His heart, what gives Him joy. We come to share His dreams and aspirations to see His kingdom come.

But God also invites us to make our requests known to Him (see Philippians 4:6). John Wesley correctly summarizes Scripture's teaching on this matter: "God does nothing but in answer to prayer."[1] It is not so much that our prayers change God's mind, although Scripture insists that they sometimes do so.[2] Prayer works because a holy and loving God has chosen to act in ways that are responsive to what His creatures do.

We do not pray because God needs our advice. Nor do we pray because God needs our company. We pray because we need God. And we pray with confidence because, as His children, we know that He desires only the best for us.

Sometimes our notions of what is best are challenged by life's experiences. Human life, even for Christians, is often marked by disappointments, failure, and suffering. Because we are not God, we do not always know what is best and we do not understand why an all-powerful God allows evil in His world, especially when we seem to be its latest victim. Still, we must not forget that submission to the Father's will meant a cross for Jesus. Nor should we forget that Good Friday was not the end of His story.

God is not an indulgent, doting Heavenly Grandfather. He knows that not everything we think we need is in our best, long-term interests. Precisely because God loves us, He allows us to experience discipline that will form our character as it did His unique Son, our Lord, who "learned obedience from what he suffered" (Hebrews 5:8).

---

1. John Wesley, *A Plain Account of Christian Perfection* (Kansas City: Beacon Hill Press of Kansas City, 1966), 108.

2. See George Lyons, "The God Who Changes His Mind," *Preacher's Magazine,* March/April/May, 1993, 30-33. Also see "Does Prayer Really Change Anything?" in *Dear God . . . Help Me Understand* (Kansas City: Beacon Hill Press of Kansas City, 1995), 92-101.

Background Scripture: Matthew 5:20; 6:5-10, 25-33; 7:7-11, 21-23; 18:19; Mark 11:17, 24; Luke 3:21-22; 9:18, 28; 11:1, 5-10; 18:1-8; 20:47; John 11:41-42; Acts 1:24; 3:1; 14:23; Romans 1:9; 8:26-27; 12:12; 1 Corinthians 14:13-19; 2 Corinthians 1:9; 12:7-10; Ephesians 1:16; 3:20; 6:18; Philippians 4:6; Colossians 1:9; 4:2; 1 Thessalonians 1:2-3; 2:13; 5:17; 2 Timothy 1:3; Hebrews 5:8; James 4:23; 1 John 3:21; 5:14-15

About the Author: Dr. George Lyons is professor of Biblical Literature at Northwest Nazarene College in Nampa, Idaho. Past president of the Wesleyan Theological Society, he is the author of *Holiness in Everyday Life* and *More Holiness in Everyday Life,* both published by Beacon Hill Press of Kansas City.

We have spent many pages in this book discussing the concepts that we can neither touch nor see. That is, by definition, the nature of our spiritual side of existence. However, we who are not only spirit but also flesh and blood have an innate desire and predisposition to study things that we can "sink our teeth into." That's why this chapter is so important in this series of topics concerning the unseen realities of our lives. When we discuss the spiritual disciplines, we enter into an arena that touches both the spiritual and the physical worlds in very tangible ways.

CHAPTER 11

Spiritual Disciplines of the Christian Life

by David W. Holdren

WHAT ARE YOUR FIRST IMPRESSIONS when you think of the word "discipline"? Maybe your mind races back to the grand old memories of being chased around the house by your mother, just before Dad came in and finished the discipline that dear old Mom intended for you. Ah yes! Some things are so *nice* to have in the past!

Discipline. That's what I just can't quite manage long enough to lose these dreadful extra pounds. I had it once, but it keeps escaping me now. I am sure it will *never* be a part of who I am. It's just not in my genes.

However, you just may beam with pride at the mere mention of the word, because you are, in fact, a disciplined person—or have become one—and your life is revealing the wonderful benefits of it. "Discipline" has become a pleasant word to you. Discipline is, indeed, a friend.

Now, ponder the phrase "spiritual discipline." What do those words do for you? For some, it represents the secure and positive walls, doors, and windows of your spiritual growth and relationship with God. For others, it suggests guilt ("I know I should"), failure ("I have started many times, only to quit just as many times"), anxiety ("God is probably pretty disappointed with me"), or dull routine ("Such things just become meaningless habits"). "Spiritual discipline" may suggest the mental picture of a saint poring over the Bible or getting into a second hour of prayer and still on a roll.

This chapter is intended to expand our horizons regarding spiritual disciplines, without overlooking some classic spiritual disciplines. We will discover that we can find practical daily benefits as we get into some disciplines that we never considered before. Let's get started on the adventure!

What's the Point?

What are the values of these things we call "spiritual disciplines"? First, they tend to be *liberating.* That's right. They tend to offer new freedom, not bondage. Any healthy discipline helps us in ways that expand our lives. I enjoy playing racquetball. My goal is to play twice a week. My discipline is to set aside two specific times and make the rest of my schedule work around those times. *But,* you may be thinking, *if you like it, it must not be a discipline.* Not true. It is a discipline because I have taken action to make sure it happens.

There are many disciplines in life that are fun, but we let the other urgencies crowd out the very things that are fun *and* important. To do the important thing, even when less important urgencies are clamoring for our attention, is a discipline. When we do those important things, it liberates our minds and attitudes. We feel good about what we have done. It helps us overcome feelings of guilt and even anxieties that become a bondage to us. Healthy disciplines liberate us.

Likewise, healthy *spiritual* disciplines liberate us. As we look into several of them, we will begin to realize how liberating they can be, on a personal level and in all of our important relationships.

Establishing spiritual disciplines helps us build *goal-oriented lives.* Study the lives of people both great and common. The ones who were the most fulfilled and made the greatest impact had goals. They made time and spent energy to achieve those goals. Discipline was required. For many, *spiri-*

tual disciplines were required. Reaching goals requires various kinds of discipline.

Disciplines lead to *progress*. Good things happen when we build disciplines into our lives. Jesus teaches us that good things happen to those who keep on asking, seeking, knocking (Matthew 7:7-8). That is a spiritual discipline. More than that, Jesus is giving us a marvelous life principle. Those who develop a passion for asking, seeking, and knocking will have a lot more of life's blessings and opportunities come to them. Christ repeatedly teaches the wisdom of discipline in managing what we have received. Carelessness, laziness, and apathy are condemned (25:14-30).

Spiritual Disciplines

Four of the classic spiritual disciplines are *prayer, fasting, study,* and *meditation.* There are others, and you may be surprised to discover what they are. For now, let's investigate these four.

Prayer is expressing ourselves to God and staying tuned in for a response. Jesus teaches us that prayer may be at its best when it is simple, sincere, and short (6:1-18).

Lots of folks think that the *discipline* of praying means it has to be long, frequent, and a pretty technical piece of work. Well, it might sometimes need to be long and frequent, but not always. It is good to schedule times for prayer, in order to have some privacy and a chance to focus our thoughts. Think of prayer as "phoning home"—checking in with ones who love us, sharing a bit of our lives, and taking time to listen.

Be aware that spiritual disciplines are not for the purpose of gaining "points" with God or even to impress others. Jesus really didn't care for that approach at all. A couple of times He really got on some folks who loved to do their ritual of praying and giving their money so everyone could see and hear them. They had huge egos. The true purpose for spiritual disciplines includes things such as helping us worship, reflect, grow, and become more Christlike.

Fasting is another spiritual discipline. Fasting may seem pretty rare, but it is not too late to learn. Fasting is the discipline of *omitting* something we like to do in order to focus on God for something more important. We tend to assume that fasting refers to food, but that is a very narrow view of it. It may be, for me, to give up one of those racquetball games and spend the equivalent time in prayer or doing something else that God has impressed upon me.

Traditionally, fasting is a kind of abstinence, to some degree, from food for some period of time in order to pray about or pray for something else. However, you may decide to engage in a kind of fasting that omits something other than food, to do something other than praying, that is nevertheless a means of seeking God or doing His work in this world.

In the Matthew 6 passage mentioned earlier, Jesus indicates that fasting is not a thing announced to the public. Do it privately, sincerely, and almost secretly, and God will reward us later!

Study is another form of spiritual discipline, usually linked to reading and studying the Bible. Many, if not most of us, stand in need of exercising this spiritual discipline. So many people tell me that time pressures and lack of comprehension are two barriers that work against this spiritual discipline. I understand. Maybe, as with prayer, amount is not the point. For beginners, find a Bible-reading guide. This gives specific portions to read that can be checked off when completed. The Bible is one of God's most basic ways of communicating to us, so we must press on to read and reflect on it.

Meditation is another little understood—and greatly misunderstood—spiritual discipline. Just because some Eastern religions or New Age adherents practice meditation, that doesn't need to spoil it for us. The real issue is about *what* we meditate on. Genesis 24:63, Psalms 1:2, 63:6, and 119:148 describe meditation methods for believers.

A basic purpose of Eastern meditation is to *empty* one's mind. In contrast, the goal of Christian meditation is to relax and free the mind in order to *fill* our senses with the goodness and glory of God. It is a kind of worship, which is one of the primary goals of all spiritual disciplines. In meditation, we find time and places where we can relax and focus on some aspect of God's work or presence in this world and in our private worlds. Meditation requires practice. The daily pace and demands of life hog so much of our time and energy that for meditation to happen, it must be on purpose. Yet, demanding times are the perfect times to discover the liberating peace and energy that emerge from Christian forms of meditation.

Are There Other Forms of Spiritual Discipline?

There certainly are! Areas such as worship, confession, celebration, and generosity are also spiritual disciplines. Why? Because they are issues of the spirit, and they touch the issues of godliness. They are not always easy or natural to do; therefore, some disciplines require effort. Makes sense, doesn't it?!

However, some of the most overlooked disciplines are the ones most related to our daily lives and activities. We mistakenly assume that spiritual disciplines are bound to become routine and mere habits, done only at certain times and places. Not always so. For example, what could be more of a spiritual discipline than what the apostle Paul describes as living in the Spirit (Romans 8:5)? This refers to the discipline of being sensitive throughout our day to the nudging and leading of God's living Spirit. This may include mustering up the spiritual discipline to battle temptation when it strikes. Or it may be the spiritual discipline of catching ourselves revealing a lousy, un-Christlike attitude, releasing a volley of nasty words, or needing to ask forgiveness of a coworker.

You might say, "Those aren't spiritual disciplines." I say they are. They are clearly spiritual issues, strongly addressed in the Bible; and it requires some serious discipline of our minds, mouths, spirits, and egos to tackle these things that are opportunities for growth in Christlikeness.

Never assume that since you may not be accomplished in

one form of spiritual discipline, you cannot be effective in exercising others.

Now, let's take one more life-changing look at spiritual disciplines that are routinely overlooked, yet affect our lives on a daily basis. The New Testament passage 2 Peter 3:11-18 serves as a biblical launching pad for several hugely important spiritual disciplines. Let's explore five of them.

Anticipation. Verses 11-14 have us "looking forward." Do you remember as a kid your anticipation of Christmas or some event that was magnificently important to you? Oh, my! The excitement and wonder was so intense and consuming that Christmas afternoon, by comparison, was a letdown.

The Bible talks about living in the present with a sense of anticipation of the new heaven and new earth (future) that God will someday bring to pass. In light of that great hope, we are encouraged to discipline ourselves to live better lives right now, as we consciously and regularly discipline ourselves to anticipate what great things God has in store for us.

Developing the spiritual discipline of anticipation requires us to wade through rivers of sorrows, climb over mountains of disappointments, and battle the daily distractions that would demand our focus only on the present, blocking from our mind the benefits of God that are sure to arrive. The text asks the question, "What kind of people should we *be* (present tense) in light of the things to come?" Positive anticipation can become a wonderful spiritual discipline that reshapes, beautifies, and strengthens life on a daily basis.

Attitude Development. In this, we find one of the keys to successful living in any age or culture. Attitudes are the ways we view life and the ways we respond to life situations, to others, and to ourselves. Attitudes are the lenses and filters through which life comes to us and through which we react. They are important on a titanic scale. Here is a true discipline for the growing Christian.

This discipline of attitude cultivation occurs in the private chambers of our minds and spirits. Discipline is also required to monitor and adjust our attitudes many times each day. It is another one of those disciplines that we take with us, never knowing just when it becomes our strength and shield or a blessing for someone else.

Besides verses 11 and 14 in our text, Ephesians 4:23 and Philippians 2:5 instruct us to seek attitudes such as Christ had and to realize that the roots of change and growth include the renewing of the attitudes of our mind. Take time to read these passages and the verses around them, noticing the awesome importance God places on attitudes.

Keeping the Peace. Ever consider *this* a spiritual discipline? Just try it. Verse 14 in the text refers to peace with God (also Romans 5:1). Other scriptures refer to having the peace of Christ (John 14:27), and yet others refer to the blessed status of peacemakers (Matthew 5:9). Keeping the peace is a gift of God's grace, in one sense, yet is also a Christian discipline of the spirit, in many ways, on many days.

Many spiritual disciplines are the kind we practice, not only in solitude or according to a schedule, but also right in the chaos of life, whenever they are needed.

Alertness. Verse 17 of our text cues us about this terrific discipline for the growing person. A sure mark of maturity is discernment and the ability to notice the approach of spiritual forces or life situations that would tend to diminish our faith, hope, love, and perseverance in Christ. That haunting phrase "I just didn't see it coming" may refer to the car that snuffed out a life or the impending breakup of a marriage. Life is distracting and often prevents us from tuning in to the persons and situations that really need our attention. Remaining alert is even the advice given to those who would be ready for our Lord's return to earth.

Some of the most beautiful thoughts in Scripture are about God's alertness to the details of our lives. "Put thou my tears into thy bottle," says one writer (Psalm 56:8, KJV). Paying attention. Observing the clues. Capturing the moment. Alertness—a magnificent spiritual discipline.

Experiencing Christ. It seems to me that this one just may be the crown jewel of all spiritual disciplines. This is the essence of Christianity. This is about passion, practicality, and everything positive in the Christian way of life. The words of the writer are, "Grow in the grace and knowledge of our Lord and Savior Jesus Christ. To him be glory both now and forever! Amen" (v. 18).

The spiritual discipline of *experiencing Christ* refers to far more, yet includes the first time we placed our personal faith in Christ as our Savior and Hope. It is learning how to follow Christ. This discipline includes a continuing thirst to know more about Christ and to appeal to His help to become more like Him. It is the spiritual discipline of pursuing Christlikeness in character and behavior. Some call this holy living.

Ephesians 5:1-2 says it this way: "Be imitators of God, therefore, as dearly loved children and live a life of love, just as Christ loved us and gave himself up for us as a fragrant offering and sacrifice to God."

This may require us to put away our former ways of life, be renewed in the attitudes of our minds, and put on the new person, created to be like God in true righteousness and holiness (see Ephesians 4:22-24).

This ultimate spiritual discipline is described by Paul in these terms: "I want to know Christ and the power of his resurrection and the fellowship of his sufferings, becoming like him in his death and so . . . attain to the resurrection from the dead" (Philippians 3:10-11).

Where from Here?

Spiritual disciplines are intended to build into our lives new passion, purpose, and power. Survey the spiritual disciplines mentioned in this chapter. Celebrate those disciplines you are already practicing. Rediscover their deeper values. Begin working on one or two that have tended to elude you. Ask for help from above. Write your intentions. Schedule some of them. But remember that some of the most essential ones are exercised right in the mainstream of your everyday experiences!

Background Scripture: Genesis 24:63; Psalms 1:2; 56:8; 63:6; 119:148; Matthew 5:9; 6:1-18; 7:7-8; 25:14-30; John 14:27; Romans 5:1; 8:5; Ephesians 4:22-24; 5:1-2; Philippians 2:5; 3:10-11; 2 Peter 3:11-18

About the Author: David Holdren is senior pastor of Cypress Wesleyan Church in Galloway, Ohio.

Next time you are in a Sunday School class or church service, take note of the percentage of prayer that is directed toward physical healing. If your church is typical, the prayer for healing seems to dominate most of our prayer sessions. Why is this so? The answer is obvious. We are needy people living in frail bodies. Sick bodies are not a desired state. Sick bodies, if left untreated, lead to the ultimate fear of all humans—death itself. Yet, is death, and the sickness that leads to it, really the ultimate fear of the human race? For the Christian there is, or should be, a higher, a more ultimate fear—the fear of forfeiting our salvation and eternal communion with God. So we are called to look again at the issue of sickness and death and to give these human conditions their proper place in our spiritual lives. Sickness and death have no claim over the Christian, for our lives are ultimately hidden in Christ. Whether we are sick or whole, whether we live or die, the important question is, "Are we serving God?" Still, sometimes God does supernaturally intervene in our lives and touch our sick bodies. Why? So we can postpone death for a few more months or years? No. God's miraculous intervention in our lives is always for one purpose—so we can better serve and glorify Him. With these thoughts in mind, let's explore the issues of healing and miracles in today's world.

CHAPTER 12

Christian Healing and Miracles

by N. Keith Hinton

IT WAS A NORMAL SUNDAY MORNING at the church. A man, weighed down with care, entered the sanctuary because a good friend had invited him. Though he almost turned around and went home before going inside, when the invitation was given, he made his way to the front and knelt awkwardly at the altar. Though he had been very far from God for most of his life, he received forgiveness for sins and his life was transformed. Something else happened that day too. God healed him of serious cancer. When I became pastor of the church a few years later, this man was on the local board and serving the Lord in good health.

A woman in our church received full use of her knee one day. God touched her even though doctors had said there was nothing they could do. Another lady was in great pain. She was diagnosed with gallstones and advised to schedule surgery. Miraculously she gained complete relief from the pain and hasn't thought about surgery for over two years.

Do you wonder if God heals today? From my own experience I would say He does.

A 28-year-old man contracted a rare form of cancer. So rare was it that only a few doctors in the country had ever tried to treat it. This guy was a fighter. His spirit was strong and his determination unwavering. He endured treatment after treatment, without much success. He was a young Christian, but he knew the church believed in healing, so he asked the church to pray. Over the next two years we prayed regularly for his healing. We laid hands on him more than once and anointed him with oil, believing that God could remove the cancer and set him free to serve His Savior in a healthy body. In spite of all we did, and contrary to what we all hoped, he died, leaving behind his wife and little girl.

Do you wonder if God always heals? From my own experience, I must say no, at least not the way we imagine He should.

Perhaps it is this apparent inconsistency, along with our desire to be disassociated with some more extreme elements of God's church, that has caused Holiness churches in more recent years largely to neglect the teaching of Christian healing. Yet, miracles and healing have always been a part of the historical church.

Though the significance of miracles—and particularly miracles of healing—has been the subject of some debate throughout the centuries, we cannot legitimately deny their existence. It is reasonable to assume that a supernatural God is still capable and likely to intervene supernaturally in the affairs of humanity, at least occasionally, if not regularly.

A Biblical Foundation

Christian healing has its roots in the Atonement. In fact, it is a basic difference in understanding the Atonement that has led to varied applications of God's Word regarding sickness and disease.

Some insist that disease, like sin, originated in the fall of the human race through Adam and Eve. Therefore sickness must have a spiritual cure as does sin. However, there are many things that we attribute to the Fall, including natural evils, thorny rose bushes, and the incompatibility of lambs and lions. No one teaches that these maladies are all to be cured by simple faith in the shed blood of Jesus and the Atonement. Likewise, though the cause of disease and sickness can be traced to humanity's fall, it really cannot be argued that God has provided the same remedy for these as He has for the universal problem of sin.

Indeed, God does heal. However, when healing takes place, it is at the discretion of a sovereign God and displays His everlasting mercy. God has not obligated himself to cure disease and sickness in the same way He has committed himself, through His Word, to forgive sin. "If we confess our sins, he is faithful and just and will forgive us our sins and purify us from all unrighteousness" (1 John 1:9). "For God so loved the world that he gave his one and only Son, that whoever believes in him shall not perish but have eternal life" (John 3:16). No such assurances exist in His Word for healing or curing all the other ills of the world that are results of the Fall. The lion *will* lie down with the lamb—but in God's good time. Though by faith individual members of the human race may experience redemption in this lifetime, the rest of God's creation cannot. Paul reminds us that "creation waits in eager expectation . . . in hope that the creation itself will be liberated from its bondage to decay and brought into the glorious freedom of the children of God" (Romans 8:19-21). There is a better world coming, but not here, not now.

The fact that God is a God of healing is an undisputed fact of Scripture. In the Old Testament God identifies himself as "the LORD, who heals you" (Exodus 15:26). There can be no denial of Christ's healing ministry in the New Testament, and the Holy Spirit is said to give "gifts of healing" to the church (1 Corinthians 12:9). In addition, if God never did anything considered miraculous again, His healing could still be seen in the incredible ability of the human body to recover from serious injury and illness because of the way He created us. He is a God of healing.

I'm convinced that all healing must be approached from a basic understanding of our relationship to God and His purpose for our lives. Our purpose is to bring glory to God. According to Romans 8:29, God's purpose is to conform us to the image of His Son. In other words, God's ultimate goal for us is that we be like Jesus and that we be saved to eternal life. Therefore, it is safe to assume that God will heal as it best serves His ultimate purpose for our lives. Faith trusts God to accomplish His purposes.

A Biblical Pattern

In James 5:7-19, we have what might be considered a pattern for dealing with the need for healing. The more familiar part of this passage concerns itself with physical sickness. "Is any one of you sick? He should call the elders of the church to pray over him and anoint him with oil in the name of the Lord. And the prayer offered in faith will make the sick person well; the Lord will raise him up. If he has sinned, he will be forgiven" (vv. 14-15). There emerges from these verses a suggested action plan.

Acknowledging need. When James writes that "he should call the elders of the church" (v. 14), he is suggesting that we must first acknowledge our need. In seeking God's intervention, there must be a confession that this problem is beyond our capability to handle it. We have a need that demands God's touch. We confess our dependency on the power of God. This is a prerequisite for many of God's promises. God often rescues us in direct response to calling on Him for help. "For he will deliver the needy who cry out, the afflicted who have no one to help" (Psalm 72:12). The psalmist testifies elsewhere, "This poor man called, and the LORD heard him; he saved him out of all his troubles" (34:6). By calling the leadership of the church together, we are acknowledging our need as well as personally initiating action that demonstrates our submission to God and His sovereign will. This submission is related to the second step.

Anointing. Second, the verse says that the church should "pray over him and anoint him with oil in the name of the

Lord" (v. 14). Since the use of oil was recognized in those days as proper medical treatment for some sickness, it would seem that this anointing with oil may serve as a reminder that God may choose to heal through the application of modern-day medicine. We must remember that medical treatment uses healing properties that God created both in our bodies and in nature. It is, therefore, proper to consider such treatment a legitimate method by which God may bring healing of our sickness.

However, there is another aspect that we cannot ignore. Oil was used in the Old Testament as a symbol of God's anointing for service and an individual's willingness to submit to God's leadership. God had kings and prophets anointed. Being God's anointed means being set apart by God to a particular area of service or ministry. When someone kneels before the Lord while the church prays for and anoints him or her with oil, the picture is very symbolic of being set apart for and submitting to God's purposes. This really is the attitude that is most exemplary of our faith.

Faith. The third part of the action plan is suggested by the words of promise "and the prayer offered in faith will make the sick person well" (v. 15). We must pray in faith. However, faith is not twisting God's arm to get what we want. Faith is discerning God's will in the situation and cooperating with Him to accomplish His will. Faith does not demand its own way but rather trusts God for His.

As an example of the kind of faith we are to have, the writer of James cites the prophet Elijah in verses 17-18. We are reminded that Elijah was just like us. We also remember that in conversation with God He had discerned God's plan and purpose both for stopping the rain and for starting it again. By his obedience and prayer, Elijah cooperated with God to accomplish God's purposes.

We must always remember that our focus is on a sovereign God who has not obligated himself to heal just because we ask Him to do so. God is not a robot or some computer reacting to the input of commands and programming. We should never imagine that we are able to manipulate God with our faith. Faith is not hurling demands in God's face, but trusting ourselves to His care.

One cannot be healed by "believing hard enough." If that were true, the power for healing would be in our minds. But it isn't. The power needed to heal is resident in God alone. When Jesus made statements such as "take heart . . . your faith has healed you" (Matthew 9:22), He did not mean that enough faith had been mustered to meet the requirements for healing, but rather that faith in Him had made it possible to carry out His will. Faith says, "Heal me or don't heal me. Either way I trust You to accomplish Your ultimate will in my life, which is my salvation and the formation of Christlike character within me."

A proper faith depends on understanding a key principle that I find represented in verse 11 of this same chapter in James. "Behold, we count those blessed who endured. You have heard of the endurance of Job and *have seen the outcome of the Lord's dealings, that the Lord is full of compassion and is merciful*" (James 5:11, NASB, emphasis added). Don't miss these words.

I am reminded of the lesson Jesus taught in Luke 18:2-8, in which an ungodly judge was persuaded by a widow's persistence to act in her behalf. This unrighteous ruler did not fear God, respect humans, or care one bit about the widow; and he was unwilling to give her assistance except to keep her from bothering him any longer. Surely, then, our loving Heavenly Father, who cares about you and me enough to put His own Son to agony on a cross, who is so attentive to the needs of His creation that not even a sparrow falls to the ground unnoticed, who loves us so much that He never slumbers or sleeps in order to focus His favor on us continually, "will not [this] God bring about justice for his chosen ones, who cry out to him day and night? Will he keep putting them off? I tell you, he will see that they get justice, and quickly" (Luke 18:7-8).

God is faithful to His children. The question is not, "Will

He act in our behalf?" That is a given. "The Lord will raise him up" (James 5:15).

The question is *when*. God will heal. However, healing is not limited to the immediate.

We often confine our thinking to the here and now. We ought to strive to keep the larger picture in mind. Christ's resurrection miracle is real. Heaven is real, and God's healing touch is real. However, sometimes, for His own reasons, God chooses to delay our healing to that time when we shall personally experience the joys of heaven and the power of our bodily resurrection. Why should that be any less miraculous than healing now? All that really matters is that our sovereign Lord is able to work His ultimate purposes in our lives.

The key is endurance. The faith that must endure, that must trust God, that still hopes and is convinced that God is true to His Word even though healing has not yet occurred, is a faith far stronger and may even be superior to the faith of a person who has seen immediate healing. When we have asked God to heal, in a proper attitude of submission and trust, we may go away convinced that He does heal in His time and in accordance with His purposes.

A Biblical Perspective

A miracle may be defined as the extraordinary intervention of God in the affairs of humanity by means not considered to be naturally occurring. A miracle, then, must necessarily be an event that takes place in addition to the broader miracles of God such as the miracle of creation itself or the miracle of His grace.

Most conservative biblical scholars would not dispute the miracle events recorded in both the Old and New Testaments. However, some would contend that the era of miracles ended with the first-century Church. Wesley suggests that the miraculous gift of healing was intended to be utilized by the Church of all ages but admits that it had largely ceased to be practiced in the Church of his day.

God is still God, and the miracle of our salvation is still the greatest miracle of all. If in the course of human history God has chosen to miraculously intervene from time to time, it should be expected that He may still do so in this present age. However, such supernatural acts of God's mercy should be viewed as additional benefits to our miraculous redemption, not as rights given to us by God with our salvation. As children, we have the privilege of asking anything of the Father. It is presumptuous, however, to expect that our desires should take precedence over His sovereign will.

Jeannie was born with spina bifida. She was expected to live only a few short days. However, she has now lived 37 years and is still going strong. Did God heal her? No, not really. Though He spared her life, she has always been confined to a wheelchair and even today is very limited in what she can do without the assistance of her family and friends.

When she was seven years old, a group of Christians asked the Father to deliver Jeannie from her disability, but He did not. For a long time Jeannie was troubled because God did not miraculously heal her body. Only recently has she begun to realize that God's delays are not God's denials. The hope of heaven's healing is not "pie in the sky" or an excuse for inferior faith; it is God's reality

Jeannie is known all over our community as an advocate for the physically challenged. She has served as a city commissioner and has recently been named by the governor of our state to fill an important agency position. The Lord is using her Christian influence in ways she never would have imagined. Our Heavenly Father has not chosen to heal Jeannie yet. So in the meantime she serves and waits for God's time and God's place.

"'For my thoughts are not your thoughts, neither are your ways my ways,' declares the Lord. 'As the heavens are higher than the earth, so are my ways higher than your ways and my thoughts than your thoughts'" (Isaiah 55:8-9).

Background Scripture: Exodus 15:26; Psalms 34:6; 72:12; Isaiah 55:8-9; Matthew 9:22; Luke 18:7-8; John 3:16; Romans 8:19-21, 29; 1 Corinthians 12:9; James 5:7-19; 1 John 1:9

About the Author: Rev. N. Keith Hinton is senior pastor of Trinity Wesleyan Church in Jackson, Michigan.

In previous chapters, we discovered that spiritual forces (both good and evil) are indeed real. An intense battle is being waged between the powers of good and evil. Yet, in the midst of the spiritual warfare taking place around us, God does not abandon us to fight alone for our spiritual survival. In fact, we must never forget that while the outcome of the skirmishes between good and evil may not be determined, the ultimate war is already won. God himself is on the side of the righteous. Righteousness will reign! God and those who serve Him in Christ Jesus will rule triumphant!

CHAPTER 13

The Power of the Holy Spirit

by Randy T. Hodges

THE SUN IS SETTING on western civilization; ominous shadows fall across politics, family life, and education. We live with a growing sense that things are winding down, and somehow freedom, justice, and order are slipping away. Scandal and scams are commonplace as men and women trade character for cash and sacrifice commitment on the altar of selfishness. Divorce, drugs, and easy sex create an environment of abuse for much of our youth. We are living on the edge of chaos. We stand on the brink of a new dark age.[1]

Are these the words of an alarmist? Is he just trying to scare us? Probably not. Living in this evil-saturated world leaves some believers feeling like bleeding guppies trying to survive in a tank of vicious piranha. Some feel as if they are about to be eaten. With more and more reports focusing on the dark side of spirituality, it's easy to fear being swallowed by the evil around us.

But the good news is that God has not abandoned or forsaken His people!

With this exciting reality in mind, we must keep this fact clear: God makes it possible for us to establish a spiritual relationship with Him. He also makes it possible for us to experience and enjoy a continuing and growing spiritual relationship—a victorious relationship that keeps progressing.

Early in His earthly ministry, Jesus encountered Satan. Scripture records the incident this way:

> Jesus, full of the Holy Spirit, returned from the Jordan and was led by the Spirit in the desert, where for forty days he was tempted by the devil. He ate nothing during those days, and at the end of them he was hungry.
>
> The devil said to him, "If you are the Son of God, tell this stone to become bread."
>
> Jesus answered, "It is written: 'Man does not live on bread alone.'"
>
> The devil led him up to a high place and showed him in an instant all the kingdoms of the world. And he said to him, "I will give you all their authority and splendor, for it has been given to me, and I can give it to anyone I want to. So if you worship me, it will all be yours."
>
> Jesus answered, "It is written: 'Worship the Lord your God and serve him only.'"
>
> The devil led him to Jerusalem and had him stand on the highest point of the temple. "If you are the Son of God," he said, "throw yourself down from here. For it is written: 'He will command his angels concerning you to guard you carefully; they will lift you up in their hands, so that you will not strike your foot against a stone.'"
>
> Jesus answered, "It says: 'Do not put the Lord your God to the test.'"
>
> When the devil had finished all this tempting, he left him until an opportune time.
>
> Jesus returned to Galilee in the power of the Spirit, and news about him spread through the whole countryside (*Luke 4:1-14*).

Three discoveries jump from this passage:

- Led by the Spirit, Jesus ventured into the desert, a lonely, threatening, and often frightening place, separated from human help and support.
- There, he faced 40 days of satanic seduction. Jesus faced the enticement to act apart from faithful depen-

dence on God—to choose a way different from what
God desired.

- At the end of the ordeal, Jesus, still living in the power
of the Spirit, stood victorious. He had not sinned, had
not succumbed to the challenge of evil.

Jesus, empowered by the Spirit, not only faced the forces
of evil but overcame them. The spiritual battle that's being
waged around us is not a seesaw battle between two equals—
God and Satan—that will determine who gets the Christian's
soul. The outcome of the war is already determined. The God
and Father of our Lord Jesus Christ reigns forever supreme.
All the forces of evil are defeated—Satan included.

Jesus withstood Satan's attempts to derail Him. Great
news awaits those of us who follow Christ today: The same
source of inner strength and power energizing Jesus then is
available to us today. When we walk in the power of the Spirit, evil does not have to triumph. We can win over evil.

"I am going to send you what my Father has promised;
but stay in the city until you have been clothed with power
from on high" (Luke 24:49). The Holy Spirit enables believers
to experience victory and to keep moving forward with God
in spiritual fellowship. In the life and words of Jesus, we discover how we, too, can establish and enjoy spiritual fellowship with God. This spiritual fellowship gives us all the help
we need to overcome the epidemic of evil surrounding us.

Let's explore together the power of the Holy Spirit that
we can experience.

Spiritual Fellowship

When we come to Christ, the Holy Spirit gives us life,
making spiritual fellowship with God possible.

Scripture makes clear what our spiritual condition is before the Holy Spirit gives us life. In his letter to the Christians
in Ephesus, Paul writes about the spiritual deadness of these
people before Christ came to their hearts:

As for you, you were dead in your transgressions

and sins, in which you used to live when you followed the ways of this world and of the ruler of the kingdom of the air, the spirit who is now at work in those who are disobedient. All of us also lived among them at one time, gratifying the cravings of our sinful nature and following its desires and thoughts. Like the rest, we were by nature objects of wrath. . . . Remember that at that time you were separate from Christ, excluded from citizenship in Israel and foreigners to the covenants of the promise, without hope and without God in the world (*Ephesians 2:1-3, 12*).

These scriptural phrases describing our spiritual condition apart from Christ should sink into our minds:

- "dead in your transgressions and sins"
- "gratifying the cravings of our sinful nature"
- "following [our sinful nature's] desires and thoughts"
- "objects of wrath"
- "separate from Christ"
- "without hope and without God in the world"
- "far away"

A dark and desperate picture of our heart is painted, isn't it? Yet through the Holy Spirit, God starts working within us even when we are in such terrible lostness, even before we come to Christ. The Holy Spirit sensitizes us to our spiritual condition—our lack of spiritual life. He awakens in us a desire for a new, living experience with God. He excites in us an inner hunger for fellowship with God. He calls us to see our sin as the spiritual death and rebellion it is and, in sorrow, to turn from it.

The New Birth

Before Christ comes to our heart, we are dead in our sins and spiritually bankrupt. There is no spiritual life in us. However, Scripture tells us what we become when the Holy Spirit brings us new life. Speaking of the new birth that the Holy Spirit makes possible, Scripture portrays a soul that is absolutely and totally transformed. When we are changed by the Holy Spirit, our moral nature is brought to life, and we take on the ability to have faith in God, to trust in Him, to love Him, and to do what He commands. These new qualities are the result of the Holy Spirit's work of regeneration within us, giving us spiritual life.

I like how one theologian describes this transformation. When regeneration occurs, "a person becomes a 'new creation . . . in Christ' (2 Corinthians 5:17). He [or she] has experienced a radical reorientation of his [or her] whole being, a reversal of values, so that what he [or she] once loved, he [or she] now hates, and vice versa. The new life in regeneration involves a dying to the old way of life and the adoption of a new way. Such a transformation of one's value system is possible only through the enabling power of the Holy Spirit."[2]

In a moment of time, when we sorrowfully repent of our sins, the Holy Spirit changes us, enabling us to become what we could never become by our own effort and striving.

A story is told that helps us see what the Holy Spirit does in our heart. A real estate agent was showing an old warehouse that had stood vacant for months. Time and weather had taken their toll. Vandals had damaged doors and broken windows. Trash was everywhere. Serious repairs were needed.

Showing the property to a prospective buyer, the real estate agent quickly pointed out that a crew could make all the needed repairs to the building. Doors could be fixed, broken glass replaced, and structural problems repaired.

"Forget the repairs," the buyer said. "When I buy this place, I'm going to build something completely different. I don't want the building; I want the site."[3]

When we try to change our lives ourselves, we take the "patch-it-up, fix-it-up" approach. It's the best we can do. These self-help changes are at best a little bandage on a gaping, lethal wound. However, when we repent of our sins and turn to Jesus for salvation, the Holy Spirit comes to our heart, saying, "I'm not here to patch up the old mess within. I've come to give you a new heart, to make you alive to God." "If anyone is in Christ, he is a new creation; the old has gone, the new has come!" (2 Corinthians 5:17).

John Wesley calls the new birth the "great change which God works in the soul when He brings it into life; when He raises it from the death of sin to the life of righteousness."[4]

When we come to Christ, the Holy Spirit gives us spiritual life, making fellowship with God possible. But there's more! Once we experience this radical transformation, God wants to help us even more.

Heart Holiness

When we experience the blessing of heart holiness, the Holy Spirit deepens our communion with God. The blessing of heart holiness is called many things—"entire sanctification," "the second blessing," "the second work of grace," "heart purity," "baptism with the Holy Spirit," and "perfect love" to name a few.

What happens when God makes us holy (sanctifies us) through and through? A modern parable may help us understand what happens in us when we are sanctified.

Having been driven for miles, the car was due for an oil change. The mechanic prepared to pour new, clean oil into the crankcase. However, before he could pour in new oil, the dirty oil, the old oil, had to be drained. He could not fill the crankcase until it was first emptied. Only when the old was purged could the fresh and clean new oil flow in.

This simple illustration points to a two-step process—cleansing and filling—that occurs in our heart as the Holy Spirit makes us holy. Before He fills us, an emptying must take place. Just as the old oil had to be drained, so too, our hearts must be purged—emptied of selfishness, of our wanting our own way, of our desires for our own self-glory. Until we are emptied of the tendency toward sin that pollutes us, the Holy Spirit himself cannot fill us.

How do believers seek the experience of entire sanctification? John Wesley points to three factors that prepare our heart for what God wants to do in us.

We must repent. This is a different repentance than takes place when we are first saved. The repentance leading to a heart made holy involves an admission that even though our sins have been forgiven and that we are indeed children of God, there still exists in us a tendency to want our way instead of God's way.

We must die to ourselves. In this process, we give up any self-perceived right to control our own life and give complete control to God. We hand over to God the keys to the control room of our heart.

We must have faith. This faith is a confidence in the promises of God to deliver us from sin and make us holy through and through.[5] These promises abound in Scripture.

> For what the law was powerless to do in that it was weakened by the sinful nature, God did by sending his own Son in the likeness of sinful man to be a sin offering. And so he condemned sin in sinful man, in order that the righteous requirements of the law might be fully met in us, who do not live according to the sinful nature but according to the Spirit *(Romans 8:3-4)*.

> I will sprinkle clean water on you, and you will be clean; I will cleanse you from all your impurities and from all your idols. I will give you a new heart and put a new spirit in you; I will remove from you your heart of stone and give you a heart of flesh. And I will put my Spirit in you and move you to follow my decrees and be careful to keep my laws *(Ezekiel 36:25-27)*.

> Since we have these promises, dear friends, let us purify ourselves from everything that contaminates body and spirit, perfecting holiness out of reverence for God *(2 Corinthians 7:1)*.

Available to All Believers

God intends this experience for all believers. A 14-year-old teen who had known Christ for 5 years was in an evening service at a summer youth camp. The evangelist preached, and God spoke to the young man's heart. When the invitation came, he went forward to yield himself completely to God. He was not sure of the terminology of holiness. His theological understanding was limited. He knew Christ was his Savior, and he wanted all God had for him. When he prayed, God responded by transforming his heart by the renewing of his mind (Romans 12:2). That happened close to 30 years ago when the Lord sanctified me.

When we become aware of our inner pollution and humbly confess our need of cleansing to God, believing that He will make us holy, then the Holy Spirit can come and fill us with His holy love. In doing so, He makes us more and more like our Lord Jesus Christ. Christlikeness is the result of a heart made holy.

A Continuing Walk

As we continue walking with God in loving obedience, the Holy Spirit increases our spiritual intimacy.

A fascinating verse closes Luke's account of the temptation of Jesus. After Satan had unsuccessfully done all he could to entice Jesus to sin, Scripture says, "When the devil had finished all this tempting, he left him *until an opportune time*" (Luke 4:13, emphasis added).

Did you catch those last words—"until an opportune time"? Satan had presently failed, but his attempt to wreck Jesus was not finished. "I am going now, but I will be back," Satan as much as threatened.

If Jesus experienced the continued temptations of Satan throughout His life, we, too, should expect to experience continuing temptation. There is never a state of grace in this life when we will be beyond temptation.

However, of greater importance is the realization that there is never a time in the Christian life when our spiritual closeness with God *must* cool, though it *may* for many reasons. Our relationship with Him can just keep getting better and better.

Scripture speaks of this continuing growth in terms of our renewal in the image of God. "And we, who with unveiled faces all reflect the Lord's glory, are being transformed into his likeness with ever-increasing glory, which comes from the Lord, who is the Spirit" (2 Corinthians 3:18).

More and more, as we walk in loving obedience, we become like our Lord himself—more and more like God. As we walk in the power of the Spirit, Christ is formed in us. Just as the Holy Spirit empowered Jesus to live victoriously over the evil around Him, so the same power of the Spirit can keep us triumphant today.

A Closing Thought

Without doubt, for many in our world today, "spirituality" has come to mean just about anything. Yet real spirituality is found in Jesus Christ. For those of us who know Jesus Christ as our Lord, the Holy Spirit's work within us is of supreme importance. We experience and enjoy real spirituality as the Holy Spirit leads us forward in a relationship with God in Christ Jesus.

---

1. Charles Colson, *Against the Night* (Ann Arbor, Mich.: Vine Books, 1991), dust jacket.

2. H. Ray Dunning, *Grace, Faith, and Holiness* (Kansas City: Beacon Hill Press of Kansas City, 1988), 449.

3. Jan L. Wilson, "New Creation," *Leadership,* Summer 1983, 95.

4. Dunning, *Grace, Faith, and Holiness,* 451.

5. Ibid., 466-67.

Background Scripture: Luke 4:1-14; 24:49; Ephesians 2:1-3, 12-13; 2 Corinthians 3:18; 5:17; 7:1; Romans 8:3-4; 12:2; Ezekiel 36:25-27

About the Author: Dr. Randy Hodges is senior pastor of First Church of the Nazarene in San Antonio.